MERSEYSIDE

Edited by Dave Thomas

First published in Great Britain in 1998 by
POETRY NOW YOUNG WRITERS
1-2 Road, Woodston,
Peterborough, PE2 7BU
Telephone (01733) 230748

Copyright Contributors 1998

HB ISBN 0 75430 227 X
SB ISBN 0 75430 228 8

FOREWORD

With over 63,000 entries for this year's Cosmic competition, it has proved to be our most demanding editing year to date.

We were, however, helped immensely by the fantastic standard of entries we received, and, on behalf of the Young Writers team, thank you.

The Cosmic series is a tremendous reflection on the writing abilities of 8-11 year old children, and the teachers who have encouraged them must take a great deal of credit.

We hope that you enjoy reading *Cosmic Merseyside* and that you are impressed with the variety of poems and style with which they are written, giving an insight into the minds of young children and what they think about the world today.

CONTENTS

Our Lady of Lourdes RC Primary School

Bethany Wilson	79
Michael Taylor	80
Estelle Smith	81
Natasha Oakley	81
Rachael Little	82
Jennifer Connaughton	82
Jamie Norris	82
Kate Stevens	82
Corinne Mellor	83
Danielle Howard	83
Christopher Thomson	83
Roua McHugh	83
Karl Hansen	84
Stacey Rodwell	84
Tom Ibison	84
Vicki Winstanley	85
Martin Thompson	85
Sophie Jagger	85
Jennifer Cox	86
Charlotte Molyneux	86
David Flynn	86
Emilia Grilli	87
Nicola Stone	87
Elizabeth Harris	87
Dean Reilly	88
Rebecca Holmes	88
Sean Ibison	88
Holly Kirby	89
Nathan Radford	89
Laurence Cox	89
Sarah Weir	90
Sam Bryce	90
Matthew Todd	90
Will Wright	91
Callum Gregson	91
Natalie Lockhart	91
Katrina Casterton	92

Rosie Burke	92
Philip Cook	92
Carly West	93
Rachel Simpson	93
James Bridge	93
Ben Sharples	93
Jenny Barton	94
Leanne Conway	94

Rainford CE Primary School

Eleanor Hopkins	94
Mandy McBlain	95
Laura Brennan	96
Tom Latham	97
Roxanne Gore	97
Danielle Simone Robinson	98
Richard Makin	98
Daniel Smith	99
Laura Preston	100
Joanna Kiddy	100
Philip Whitby	101
Rachel Large	101
Andrew Lyon	102
David Stove	102
Christopher Crichley	103

St Alban's RC School, Wirral

Catherine Brady	103
Rachael Clay	104
Marcus Smith	105
Katie Melling	105
Matthew Wilson	105
Jenny Meyers	106
Sarah Lowndes	106
Michelle White	106
Sara Lynch	107
Christina O'Brien	107
Lisa Fadden	108

Emma Vose	127
David Carroll	127
Jenny Ardrey	128
Michael Arrowsmith	128
Heather Winstanley	129
Susan Cairns	129
Lewis Harris	130
Helen Rothwell	130
Jodie Coughlan	131
Tom Coghlan	131
Phillip Brougham	132
Anthony Freeman	132
Holly McCarthy	133
Thomas Meredith	134

St Joseph's RC Primary School, Wallasey

Claire Latham	134
Ellen McGinley	135
Gemma Morton	136
James McGowan	137
Michael Davies	138
Bradley McGovern	138
Barry Murphy	139
Richard Palin	139
Billy Hopkins	140
Natalie Lucas	140
Sean Charlesworth	141
Sarah Griffiths	142
Alexander Breen	142
Jenna Price	143
Andrew Parry	144
Beckie Cleary	144
Christopher King	145

St Laurence's RC Primary School, Kirkby

Christian Thomas	146
Jonnie Brennan	147
John Campbell	148

Rachael Delic	167
Emma Cookson	167
Melanie Hughes	168
Mandy Shanks	168
Howard Hughes	169
Helena Seddon	169
Laura Telfer	170
Adam Churchill	170
Jennie Mandelkow	170
Catherine Nixon	171
Jonathan Edwards	171
Rachael Karran	171
James Edwards	172
Jack Barrett-Rosindale	172
Craig Hallam	173
Stephanie Wrennall	173
Nicky Aspinwall	174
Lindsey Willis	174
Kyndra McKinney	175
Roisin McIvor	175
David Pope	176
Lucy Wathan	176
Amy Begley	177
Gavin Jones	177

St Teresa's RC Primary School, St Helens

Kerrie Jones	178
Mark McNicholas	178
Alison Waring	179
Helen Alexander	179
Clare Owen	180
Mathew Taylor	180
Liam Jones	180
Daniel Brown	181
John Worthington	181
Kirsty Holden	181
Natasha Roberts	182
Gary Donnelly	183

Dannielle Helsby	183
Kerrie Johnson	184
Alison Hatton	184

St Winefride's Juniors, Bootle

Andrew Seagraves	185
Stephen Ford	186
Frankie McKeon	186
Stephanie Evans	187
Daniel Sullivan	187
Jayne Tomley	188
Craig Graham	188
Sarah Groom	189
Kerry Jones	189
Chelsea Cousins	190

Shoreside Primary School

Philip Lennon	190
Steven Forshaw	191
Emma Chandley	192
Harriet Aitken	192
Jenny Hearnshaw	193
Hannah McBride	194
Gary Menzies	194
Martha Sprackland	195
Jenna McKenna	195
Jenny Owen	196
Daniel Trickett	196
Bryony Beale	197
Jenna Davidson	197
Adam Cadwell	198
Anne Marie Watson	198
Daniel Green	199
Philip Ratcliffe	199
Rhona Morris	200
Michael Hall	200
Jenna Gavin	201
Stephanie Jayson	201

Alexandra March	202
Matthew Dent	202
Edward Greenwood	203
Michael Scholfield	203
Andrew Rea	204
James Fitzgerald	204
Hannah Brownlow	205
Andrew Dodson	205
Maximilian Bienkowski	206
Jennifer Gorrell	206

Stanney Grance CP School

Scott Jewkes Keating	207
Karen Duffin	207
Sam Fry	208
Claire Hall	209
Abigail Jones	210
Nikki Mather	210
Kelly Dinkerley	211
Jodie Seymour	211

Thornton Hough Primary School

Nicholas Wood	212
Gordon Farquhar	213
William Parry-Jones	214
Christopher Hulley	214
Christopher Wood	215
Stuart Webb	215
Sarah Taperell	216
Michael Hopkinson	216
Thomas Richardson	217
Sam Pringle	217
David Griffiths	218
Matthew Davies	218
Sarah Warburton	219
Hayley Dineley	219
Michael Kenworthy	220
Christopher Williams	220

THE POEMS

THE STORM

The sky goes dismal and dark
and prepares itself for a nightmare.
The rain starts to hit the floor
like a marching army.
Thunder like a banging drum,
lightning like an electric spark.
Howling, deafening, wild,
Reaching a crescendo and climax.
The sky awakes from its nightmare.
A rainbow forms - there's
            Peace again!

Stephanie Smith (9)
Evelyn County Primary School

MORNING

The sun rises like some fireworks.
People rushing to work.
The smell of toast.
The shops opening.
The milkman coming.
The dew sparkling.
The day is here!

Rachel Bushell (8)
Evelyn County Primary School

NIGHT

Night is a monster
Hunting and killing
Silver with black eyes
The sky like a tail that never ends
The moon like a huge black in the world
The wolves howling on hills
The barking of bulldogs
Night is gloomy and waving and never ending.
Bang! The night fades away!

Tom Clarke (9)
Evelyn County Primary School

MORNING

The sun rises
Like a fireball,
The smell of hot buttered toast,
The alarm roaring like a lion,
See people rushing like *mad!*
And the milkman whistling along,
The morning has come.

Victoria Waters (9)
Evelyn County Primary School

THE STORM

The dark and gloomy clouds cave in.
Buckets and buckets of rain splatter down
from the clouds.
Suddenly there is a big crashing noise
and then a big bang.
The lightning brightens up the dark sky
with brilliant flashes.
The rain begins to trail off and the lightning
fades away and peace comes to the sky.

Simon Evans (8)
Evelyn County Primary School

WHO AM I?

I can sink a ship in the roaring sea,
Crashing, whipping, screaming.
I can ruffle your hair gently,
Gusting, sighing and wailing.
I can rattle the bin lids,
Angry, powerful, banging.
Who am I?
The powerful and wonderful wind.

Gillian Lysons (9)
Evelyn County Primary School

NIGHT

Night is a huge black panther
Leaping and roaring.
Ebony-black with twinkling yellow eyes.
Its fur like a huge blanket.
Its eyes like candles.
The squeaks of rats.
Night is mysterious and magic.
Oh no! It swallowed me!

Stephanie Marr (9)
Evelyn County Primary School

WHO AM I?

I can growl and snatch
      Shrieking, flapping, gusting
I can carry the scent of flowers
      Creeping, whispering, fluttering
I can strip all the leaves off an oak tree
      Wailing, crashing, yelling
          Who am I?
The strong, powerful wind.

Gemma Gerrard (9)
Evelyn County Primary School

MARS ATTACK

You will think I am making this up you know
But it really happened.
An alien came down from space,
And took me up to Mars.
But all they said is
'Mars attack, Mars attack.'
I just stood there feeling glum,
But then I thought Mars quite tasty but
I still prefer Lion bars.
The oldest alien said
'What are you thinking about?'
I said 'Have you got a Lion bar
Or even a Snickers bar?'
He just looked at me in a funny way
And walked off the other way.
I was starting to get a little hungry
And asked if I could go home.
I had a little trouble,
Because he did not understand.
I asked another, he said 'Yes,'
He took me home that very day.
You don't believe me do you?
But it did happen.

Rebecca Hansen (9)
Gayton Primary School

I WENT UP TO SPACE

I got up in the morning
My little brother snoring
Now we're going, now we're going
I went up to space
A really ugly face
Popped up, popped up
I think he wants a fight
I'm getting out of sight
Now we're dead, now we're dead
A planet came whizzing
It was popping and fizzing
Let's get away, let's get away
I think that was Mars
I liked the stars
They're pretty, they're pretty
I think I'd like to go
Moaned my little bro'
Okay we're going, okay we're going
One more look in space
No more ugly face
We are going, we are going.

Ashleigh Bemrose (8)
Gayton Primary School

COSMIC

C omets racing through the sky
O uter space dark and misty
S hooting stars see them shine
M ars glooming red and hot
I lluminated sky
C lusters of stars floating about.

Michelle Afaleq (8)
Gayton Primary School

METEORITE

Meteorite, meteorite
flying through the air.
Meteorite, meteorite
I saw it there.
Meteorite, meteorite
falling there, there, there!
Meteorite, meteorite
where, where, where?
I told my friend but
he didn't believe me.
I told my sister but she
didn't believe me.
I told my dad but he
didn't believe me.
I told my mum but
even she didn't believe me.
I don't think anybody
will believe me so I will
keep it as one *big* secret.

Christopher Lewis (9)
Gayton Primary School

SPACE

There is something called space
That looks like a face
Space is round
But has never been found
What colour is space?
Maybe it's dark like night
Or maybe it's bright like day.

Guy Wilton (8)
Gayton Primary School

THE COSMIC GALAXY

Way out there
Beyond the skies,
The cosmic stars
Go flying by.

The Moon is bright,
At first sight,
Mostly not at day,
But night.

The planets soundless
In the sky,
Watch meteors
Go flying by.

The comets whizz,
And fly around,
All night long
Without a sound.

Katie Lea (8)
Gayton Primary School

SPACE, SPACE A COSMIC RACE

Space space a cosmic race
            With the Sun and stars
                    Jupiter and Mars.
Spacemen flying through the air
            Rockets crashing everywhere.
Little aliens in the air
            Driving, crashing everywhere.
Oh no - there, there!

Ryan Edwards (9)
Gayton Primary School

LOOK OUT, ALIEN ABOUT

There was a little alien,
Who lived on Mars,
You wouldn't believe it,
But he was mad on cars.

Then one day,
He took a test,
To show everyone,
He was the best.

The little alien,
Got in a fix,
And ended up,
On Planet Twix.

The poor little thing,
Our friend the alien,
Turned out to be
A total failien!

Robyn Green (9)
Gayton Primary School

COSMIC

Black holes
became fashionable
when Stephen Hawkings came to be
because scientists said that's how life should be.
So we travelled past Mercury and Venus,
Mars, Earth, Jupiter, Neptune
and Uranus to
love!

Kathleen Malkin (9)
Gayton Primary School

THE BIG BANG!

All the planets,
Out in space,
Have a place,
By God's decree.
If it wasn't
For the big, big
     Bang!
No one would be born.
So now we say that the
Big Bang made us!
The world, Jupiter and Mars,
As well as little stars,
We're all made from the
     Big, big, big
        Bang!

Sarah Hutchings (8)
Gayton Primary School

COSMIC

Oh no, there goes my custard pie,
Floating in the sky.
It looks like it is waving goodbye.
Duck, a shooting star,
Wow, a planet.
I can see it afar.
There is a bright light
Is it a baboon?
Oh no, it is just the moon.

Olivia Hewitt (9)
Gayton Primary School

OUTER SPACE

In outer space,
planets everywhere,
we're on a case,
so aliens beware.

> In outer space,
> watch out shooting stars,
> for the human race,
> little aliens on Mars.

UFOs flying across the air,
the aliens crashing,
but they don't care.

Christopher Allen (9)
Gayton Primary School

COSMIC AND SPACE

Cosmic, cosmic whizzing round the moon
Just like a rocket about to go boom!

Cosmic, cosmic whizzing round space
Just like an alien in the human race!

Cosmic, cosmic as hot as the sun
Just like an alien having a lot of fun!

Cosmic, cosmic whizzing round the universe
Then it bounced off Mars whizzing round the stars
that sent it far far away just to play.

Daniel Mcgenity (8)
Gayton Primary School

INTO SPACE

I went up in a rocket,
Nothing was the same,
Someone called my name!
I looked out of the window,
I saw a bright green face.
Then it went.
Look there's Jupiter and Mars,
A planet and some stars.
Now I've landed on a planet,
I wonder if it spins - can it?
I'm fed up with space,
I want the human race.

Emma Hutchings (8)
Gayton Primary School

BANG!

Way out in
   Space
One day
There was a
   Bang!
It made
   Mars
   Jupiter
   Saturn and
   lots of other
   planets too.

Sarah Gibbs (8)
Gayton Primary School

SOME OLD, SOME NEW, SOME THE SAME

It was cold . . .
When I was young
We used to build igloos
With a hole in the top.
We used to go and hunt.
It was cold.
We used husky dogs.
When blizzards came
We entertained ourselves
By making soapstone figures.

Now they use log cabins
And snowmobiles
And raised houses and fires.
It is cold and they have a big pipeline.
It is cold.
All that oil has ruined the environment.
It is cold.
It is surrounded by stainless steel.
It is cold.
It kills all the animals.
It is cold.

I prefer the old way do you?

Phil Jacob (9)
Great Meols Primary School

DUNKIRK - THE SOLDIER

He sees, people getting killed,
Bombs blazing beyond the hills,
Fires frizzling and falling bodies,
People praying for injured friends.

He hears, the crackling of fires,
People screaming for help,
Explosions,
Bangs, booming screaming battlers.

He tastes, burning ashes,
Salt as he licks his dry lips,
He touches, dead friends,
He feels his hands perspiring
as he grips his gun.

He smells, the choking smell of
burning,
The sea with ship sailing slowly
away.

He feels, overcome by claustrophobia,
homesick
and petrified and scared,
he thinks of home,
as he stares longingly out to sea.

Nick Van Miert (11)
Great Meols Primary School

MY ROAD

When
you
go
down
my
road
you
will
find
my
abode.
Outside
my
house
are
blossom
trees
which
are
losing
their
petals
in
the
breeze.

Gemma Mitchell (10)
Great Meols Primary School

IN A FOREST

Calm, all alone, locked up in my dreams

In a forest
leaves fluttering,
flowing gently down -
gold, yellow, green
like butterflies in the breeze,
as trees sway
from side to side,
the river running by.

In a forest,
leaves fluttering,
twisting, turning,
swirling, whirling,
like pieces of silk,
as the breeze blows them
into the water,
the river running by.

In a forest,
leaves fluttering,
dancing and tossing,
shaking, shaking,
flashes of colour,
dying on the ground,
the river running by.

Calm, all alone, locked up in my dreams.

Joseph Gillespie (8)
Great Meols Primary School

GROVE PARK RABBITS

A little girl steps out of her house,
Her father following close behind her.
They walk towards their car.
He presses a button,
The doors open.
They climb in.
He presses a button,
The doors close.
He turns a knob on the steering wheel,
He types in a code.
The automatic car drives off,
On its own.
They reach a place,
A place they used to call Grove Park.
Now it no longer holds that title,
For it is the height of technology,
With its electric swings and climbing frame.
They step out of the car,
Onto the cold, hard metal pavement.
They enter the park.
Suddenly, the girl cries out in horror,
'What's that?
Dad, there!'
Her father takes out his gun.
Bang! Bang! Bang!
Gone.
The last rabbit on Earth,
Gone.

Amy Allen (11)
Great Meols Primary School

THE MERSEY

I am the Mersey,
I run through towns and villages,
I see things that you don't know about,
I know things that you don't care about.

Stop polluting my water,
Stop writing on the walls,
Stop stealing,
Stop bullying.

Forget all the bad things,
Think about the good things,
There's lots of good things if you think,
Like friends and family,
Air to breathe, things like that.

Enjoy what you have around you,
Don't spoil our friendship circle,
See the need of others.

On my way to other towns,
I see boats sailing,
Happy people caring,
Mean people killing things.

Happy people talk and laugh together,
Mean people trapping things,
God made the world for us to look after,
Not to go and spoil it.

I am the Mersey,
I run through towns and villages,
I see things that you don't know about,
I know things that you don't care about.

Rachel Parry (9)
Great Meols Primary School

KILLER ON THE LOOSE

In the water a figure creeps,
A figure which lies,
And quietly sleeps.

Then one eye opens,
The other one closed,
The open one grows wider,
The second one posed.

The ghostly body
Lies on the seabed,
Now he's hungry,
He wants to be fed.

Then he comes,
Making a splash,
Then blood flies,
In a flash.

Now he's gone down
To the seabed,
This treacherous beast
No longer needs to be fed.

Adam Morgan (8)
Great Meols Primary School

IF ONLY I WAS A CAT

I come along for spiders, mice, cats, dogs and rabbits,
They run away and run into houses making people very mad.
I am a black cat.
I am creepy and scary.

Craig Kell (9)
Great Meols Primary School

MERSEYSIDE

A cheer,
A roar,
Liverpool have just scored.
Another cheer,
Another roar,
Everton have scored four.
Keegan,
Dalgleish,
What a pair if they stayed here at Liverpool.
I wonder what a team Liverpool could be with Dixie Dixie Dean.

A swish,
A sway,
Boats all over the River Mersey.
A ferry stops at Seacombe to go to the aquarium,
The Liver Birds look like they're flying free.
A bang,
A boom,
The Mersey starts to zoom.

Granada Television is at the Albert Dock filming,
A shame not to be there.
Everyone rushes to get into the Museum,
Whilst at the art gallery it's calm and peaceful.

Cycling is a great sport, especially when Chris Boardman is from
                                        Merseyside,
But if you go through the tunnel you'll discover,
Birkenhead,
Or Wallasey.

A screech,
A scratch,
A plane zooms into the air.
The horse racing is around at Aintree,
Red Rum zooming around,
And then in a flash of light he was gone,
But his spirit still lives on.

Adam Franks (11)
Great Meols Primary School

THE FOX-HUNT

I am a fox,
Resting in the grass,
Suddenly I hear a sound,
The hunt.

I jump up quickly,
And race through the trees,
I hear the hounds yelping, calling to the breeze,
The hunt.

The hounds are gaining,
I can feel their breath upon my flanks,
Snap!
I feel a pain in my thigh,
The hunt.

Suddenly the hounds are upon me,
I feel a bite to my throat,
I feel my life fading away,
The hunt.

Laura Buckberry (10)
Great Meols Primary School

THE HOYLAKE LIFEBOAT

Green, blue, thrashing, rough,
        cold, deep, dirty and brown,
Green, blue, thrashing, rough,
        cold, deep, dirty and brown,

The lifeboat launches zooming along,
through the waves so fast and strong,

Green, blue, thrashing, rough,
        cold, deep, dirty and brown,
Green, blue, thrashing, rough,
        cold, deep, dirty and brown,

The lifeboat men see the flare
floating down over there,

Green, blue, thrashing, rough,
        cold, deep, dirty and brown,
Green, blue, thrashing, rough,
        cold, deep, dirty and brown,

The boat is sinking under the waves,
people are hoping they might be saved,

Green, blue, thrashing, rough,
        cold, deep, dirty and brown,
Green, blue, thrashing, rough,
        cold, deep, dirty and brown,

So exhausted the people climb out,
they're much too tired to look about!

Green, blue, thrashing, rough,
        cold, deep, dirty and brown,
Green, blue, thrashing, rough,
        cold, deep, dirty and brown,

The lifeboat turns and speeds away,
frothing waves are here to stay,

Green, blue, thrashing, rough,
        cold, deep, dirty and brown,
Green, blue, thrashing, rough,
        cold, deep, dirty and brown,

Back in the harbour people cheer,
thanks for returning them safely here.

Green, blue, thrashing, rough,
        cold, deep, dirty and brown,
Green, blue, thrashing, rough,
        cold, deep, dirty and brown.

Richard Hoyle (9)
Great Meols Primary School

SUN

Yellow,
  gold,
    red,
      orange is the sun.
Silver,
  white,
    the sun is all different colours.
The sun gives us warmth
and makes the flowers grow.
The sun is the morning because
it brightens up the sky.
When the night breaks in
the
  sun
    begins
      to
        die.

Jessica Brooks (8)
Great Meols Primary School

NEVER BUY A HOUSE AT MUTTERIN LANE

Never buy a house at Mutterin Lane -
All the kids screamin' and shoutin' is a pain.
The houses are such a terrible sight
and all the burglars come at night.

Never! buy a house at Mutterin Lane -
it certainly costs enough.
The neighbours aren't friendly,
They are angry and tough!

Never buy a house at Mutterin Lane -
All the people who live here would drive you insane.
It's dirty, noisy and very loud,
but all the people who live here think it's sound.

Never! buy a house at Mutterin Lane -
There's an awful smell from the drain.
There's rats and mice and cockroaches too,
I'd never ever live there, would you?

Liam Murphy (10)
Great Meols Primary School

DAFFODIL

Nice, beautiful, pretty, gorgeous daffodil.
Standing in the sun.
Showing off with pride.
He has great power and strength.

Alexandra Cawthorne (8)
Great Meols Primary School

JOURNEY ACROSS THE MERSEY

I'm going on a ferry on a journey across the Mersey.

I can see on the river, with boats sending toys,
Seagulls bobbing up and down, as well as the buoys,
On a journey across the Mersey.

I can see around me, the Liver Birds and all,
The cargo ships going in and out
And some boys playing with a ball,
On a journey across the Mersey.

I can see on the ferry,
People being merry,
As we end our journey,
Our journey across the Mersey.

Now I have finished my journey,
My journey across the Mersey.

Andrew Coulson (10)
Great Meols Primary School

MY HANDS

My hands can hurt, live, smash, grab, feel,
touch, make, play, break, take, flap,
open, dance, carry, move, work, close,
write, hug.
That is what my hands can do!

Charlotte Lomax (8)
Great Meols Primary School

THE LAME BOY IN THE PIED PIPER OF HAMELIN

I heard the pipe and just couldn't resist it.
As I was following it, we came to a hill. Up we went.
As we were following, he explained where we were going.

'Rushing rivers flowing by,
Bees with no sting in the sky.
Sparrows like peacocks sing,
Horses with eagle's wing.'

In a few minutes we came to a mountain.
As we came up to it, it opened.
I had a broken leg, I couldn't catch up.
When they were in, the mountain closed.
The piper was already out.
Where were my friends?
I told the town the story.
Their faces, dull and grey.

Laura Cubbin (8)
Great Meols Primary School

ICE

Cold, ice-cold hands
Me frozen, people cold
Snowflakes falling
Slippery, you fall over
And you freeze.

Luke Meadows (8)
Great Meols Primary School

THE PLAYGROUND

I come zooming
Out of the door!
Rushing to the others.
Sometimes I am on Joseph's side
Sometimes I am not.
I dodge people,
I dodge, I run,
I twist, I twirl,
I turn around,
I look for a gap,
Hurray!
I have made it to
the other side of the playground.
Hurray!
So it goes on and on . . .
Till the bell goes.

Ashley Rogan (8)
Great Meols Primary School

SPRINGTIME

Daffodils dancing in the spring
Bright and yellow and shining
Bluebells bobbing up and down
Nice and peaceful not a sound
Spring is here all around
It is spring, spring, spring.

Gabriella Torpey (8)
Great Meols Primary School

BONFIRE NIGHT

Listen to the sparklers *hissssssssing*
Listen to the bonfire crackling
Listen to the firework banging
Listen to the Catherine wheel screaming
Listen
Boom! Bang! Whooosh!
Screech! Eeeee! Hissssss! Scream! Whistle!

Colin Wagstaff (9)
Great Meols Primary School

A SOLDIER OF THE SOMME

Roaring, raging rifles clattered, a lonely soldier
had been hit and lay defenceless on the ground.
He listened to all the bangs and booms of the
shells and guns around. He heard the sounds
and screams of people dying one by one.
He stayed and listened, waiting for help,
but no one came and his life was gone.

Craig Randles (11)
Great Meols Primary School

THE SUN

I am the sun
I don't like the wind
The wind blows me up and down
When it starts to rain
The sun goes down drip drop
Puddles round me on a cold night.

Hannah McCormick (9)
Great Meols Primary School

THE PRIDE OF MERSEYSIDE

Driving,
        driving along Anfield Road,
Driving,
        driving right up to the gates of Liverpool,
Driving,
        driving right into a parking space,
Walking,
        walking into the stadium,
Paying,
        paying to get in,
Sitting,
        sitting watching the match,
Scoring,
        Scoring *John Barnes!*
Scoring is the best.

Sam Favager (11)
Great Meols Primary School

THE SUN

The Sun is down and it pops up.
'Come on, wake up' says the Sun.
It's morning already.
'Yes, come on, don't waste the day,
It's nearly the end of summer.'
Oh no! I'd better get up.
Oh no!, It's dark and the Sun is going down.
I have missed the Sun.

Jack Brooks (8)
Great Meols Primary School

THE WIRRAL

North, south, east and west - Wirral living is the best.
　　Ferries and ships, I look at the sea,
　　　　Soon I'll be across the Mersey.
　　　　　Come and play or sail away,
　　　　　　You can rest another day.

Summertime by the sea, walking with my family.
　　I ride my bike along the prom,
　　　　Counting the seagulls one by one.
　　　　　Soon I will be tired, I guess,
　　　　　　So I'll stop for an ice-cream, and have a rest.
　　　　　　　The sun is setting in the sky
　　　　　　　　So from me and my poem -
　　　　　　　　　It's bye bye.

Bianca Maraney (8)
Great Meols Primary School

ICE-COLD

I am in a cloud,
looking down,
Oh, oh, here I go.
Brrr!
I am off, landing in a gutter.
Oh no, I'm freezing,
I am an icicle.
Brrrrrrr!

Michael Sherlock (8)
Great Meols Primary School

LIVERPOOL VS EVERTON

In a boat 1, 2, 3,
say hello to Liverpool
and the pier head
Say bye bye to Birkenhead.

In a car 1, 2, 3,
going down Anfield Road,
hearing the crowd cheer and roar
say bye bye to my front door.

In the stand 1, 2, 3,
Steve McManaman scored again,
the fans chant and stamp
say bye bye to Everton.

Elliot Jones (10)
Great Meols Primary School

OH FOR A TRAP, A TRAP, A TRAP

His eyes are like pinballs.
Where does he come from?
He's strange!
He has light, loose hair.
His skin is swarthy.
His cloak is half red and half yellow.
Who is he?

He's the Pied Piper of Hamelin!

Kate McCormick (8)
Great Meols Primary School

WHEN I CLOSE MY EYES

When I close my eyes,
I am . . .
Riding on a dolphin's back
Through the splashing waves,
Swimming under the sea,
The fish and all the colours,
Exploring a secret cave,
Finding lots of treasures.
When I open my eyes,
I am no longer doing any of these.
But I can always close my eyes,
Again and again and . . .
Again.

Stephanie Hatton (10)
Great Meols Primary School

HARVEST

Harvest is a pleasant time,
When you can see the corn,
With lots of fruits and vegetables,
Go pick some and enjoy.

Go and make a corn doll,
Go and pick some corn,
Put a headdress on her head,
And make her a shawl.

Lynsey Forber (10)
Great Meols Primary School

THE ROLY-POLY BIRD

Once there was a roly-poly bird.
Who liked to roll in lemon curd.
The lemon curd was really sticky
And so he got a little icky.

The icky sticky roly-poly bird.
I'm sure you children have all heard
Rolled all the way down the hill
Until he felt a little ill.

He spied a little stream nearby
And without stopping to ask why
He jumped in and said goodbye!

Jonathon Cannon (9)
Great Meols Primary School

TIGER

Tiger growling, tiger hunting.
Creeping through the bush.
The tiger is stripy.
The tiger is fierce.
Tiger please do hush!
Look after your cubs Mrs Tiger
A hunter is nearby.
Tiger growling, tiger hunting.
Creeping through the bush.

Niamh Hogan (8)
Great Meols Primary School

BEHIND THE CLOSED DOOR

At the end of the hall in our brand-new house,
I can hear a scratching scuttling noise
behind the closed door
in the hall.
It's a scary spooky room, the only scary one,
I don't understand, I really don't.
The noise seems to be coming from underneath the floor.
It can't be a mouse, it's more like a clutter,
A mouse just seems to pitter-patter.
It can't be a rat, it's still too quiet,
But on the other hand maybe, it could be a monster,
Or it's just me being silly and my imagination running away with me.

Louise Maddocks (10)
Great Meols Primary School

THE TERRIBLE TROUBLESOME THREE

They hurt me in the playground, they think it's really funny,
They pinch me in the dinner hall, and take away my money.

They break up all the pencils, even in the class,
They always push in line and they push me till I'm last.

They scribble in the reading books, sometimes write my name,
So Miss finds out and I always get the blame.

They tear up all the paper and always blame it on me,
I hate being bullied by the terrible troublesome three.

Chloe Byatt (9)
Great Meols Primary School

SPIDERS

Spiders, spiders,
small and grey.
I'm trapping flies
all day.
Spiders spinning
a web
in a circle.
All their thread comes
out of their bodies.
Help! I've been
caught in a
spider's web.

Charlotte Gregory (8)
Great Meols Primary School

MERSEYSIDE GLORY

Merseyside is the place to be,
If you like the air, land and sea.
Food to eat and water,
Animals all over the place,
Plants and trees that look nice,
People everywhere in buildings, and electricity,
Everywhere.
Birds in the sky,
Fishes in the sea,
Won't you come along and see it all with me?

Emily Winters (10)
Great Meols Primary School

THE WIND ALWAYS BLOWS

The wind can blow down a tree,
Or even some honey from a bee.
The wind can make lots of waves,
Or even blow for a couple of days.
The wind can blow off my hat,
Or even blow over a pussy cat.
The wind once blew off my roof,
And nicked a little horse's hoof.
It can blow down a little house,
Or blow away a tiny mouse.
Oh hurrah, the wind has gone away,
But it will come back another day.

Alistair Hough (8)
Great Meols Primary School

THE RAIN COMES TUMBLING DOWN

The rain comes tumbling down,
The rain makes the sun frown,
The rain splashes on the ground,
Running to the rivers, all around.
The rain splashes down Merseyside,
And runs to the waves, and the tide.
When the rain gets very wet,
You'll get soaked I bet I bet!
When the rain dies and up comes the sun,
Everywhere is dry and the rain is gone.

Kristian Baldock (9)
Great Meols Primary School

RAINBOW

See the colours of the rainbow
glisten in the sky,
the sun sets for the evening
the rainbow's going to die.
You know at the end of the rainbow
there's always something nice,
at sunrise in the morning
the rainbow appeared in a trice.
I know that the rainbow
is fading away in the sky,
so evening good morning
and rainbow goodbye.

Jessica Broadbere (8)
Great Meols Primary School

BONFIRE NIGHT

Snap! Crackle! Pop!
A firework whizzes by.
Boom! Screech! Scream!
Brightens up the sky!

Whizzing, spinning, sticky toffee,
Babies crying,
Cups of coffee!
Baked potatoes, burgers too,
Fireworks spinning,
People say *'Ooh!'*

Fay Scott (9)
Great Meols Primary School

THE WIND

The wind is flowing through my house,
The leaves are slowly fluttering to the ground,
The wind is slightly whistling,
Then *bang! Crash!*
The door is crashing against the wall
and keeping me awake.
The wind is so strong it is knocking the trees.
It is knocking on my window
It is ready to get me.
I am scared, it is whistling and whirling
and twisting and turning.
Bang! Crash! Wallop!

Jessica Dixon (8)
Great Meols Primary School

A DRAGON FOR A PET

My dragon is not
very big, but
not very small.
Only I can see
my dragon.

Some people
may think it's boring.
But I think
it is very appalling
to think my dragon is boring.

Jonathan Jones (9)
Great Meols Primary School

CHOCOLATE!

I like chocolate, I think it's yummy,
But I like it best when it's in my tummy.
I like chocolate ice-cream,
I like chocolate sauce,
And in the farm nearby
there's a chocolate coloured horse.

I like chocolate breakfast,
and chocolate eggs too.
I like it when my fingers are covered in goo.
I like chocolate, I think it's yummy,
But I like it best when it's in my tummy!

Elizabeth Gill (9)
Great Meols Primary School

ICE-COLD

Alaska - cold, boggy, soggy
Oil spills, seals killed
Alaska - nippy snow, snowball fights
Alaska - the people used to build igloos
with a hole at the top.

Alaska - polar bears stomped along
Alaska - snow as white as white can be
Alaska - snowmobiles slide along on the snow
to Iceland - *Whoosh!*
Alaska.

Todd Byrom (9)
Great Meols Primary School

THE LADY OF SHALOT
LOOKING THROUGH THE MIRROR

Birds, some twitter some flitter,
some fly and some swoop.
Each little bird
has its own magic power.
Some have beauty,
some have strength.
All are free but I am not.
Through the mirror shadows walk.
I'm looking into a pool of dirt, mist and fog.
Life to me is nothing, meaningless.

Tori Warren (10)
Great Meols Primary School

MY MATE

My mate is,
weird, but I don't care.

My mate is,
sometimes horrible, but I don't care.

My mate,
sometimes gets on my nerves, but I don't care.

I like my mate very much, whatever she is like.
You see, I don't care what my mate is like,
she is still my friend.

Ceri Walker (10)
Great Meols Primary School

SNOW

I wake up the next day
very excited because it is Christmas.
I open my window and say
'It's Christmas and it is snowing!'
I wake up my dad and tell him it is snowing.
He gets dressed and goes outside.
We pack some hot drinks
and some cookies in a black sack.
We were in the garden all day long.
We made a snowman.
At the end we went to bed very early and tired.

Aimee Harding (8)
Great Meols Primary School

AUTUMN COLOURS

Golden yellow.
Copper.
Dazzling red.
Burnished gold.
Burnt orange.
Muddy brown.
Berry red.
Purple berries.
Fiery scarlet.
Iron-grey skies.
Autumn colours.

David Rampling (8)
Great Meols Primary School

WIND

Wind whistling
wind swirling
wind cold
wind blowing
wind is the wind
so let it be our
whistling
swirling
cold
blowing
wind!

Lauren Mitchell (8)
Great Meols Primary School

CALENDAR RHYME

January is very cold,
February, cold winds get told,
In March the flowers begin to grow,
April comes hot and low,
In May the roses are red,
In June the farmers go to bed,
In July the sun shines,
In August there are lots of wines,
September, the leaves turn brown,
October winds blow down town,
November fills with fear and smear,
December comes and ends the year.

Liam Fillingham (8)
Heswall County Primary School

CALENDAR RHYME

January, the first month of the year.
The days are dark and cold.

February, the month of love.
The days are longer.

March, spring is in the air.
The bulbs are growing.

April, when the trees are in bud.
The Easter bunny arrives.

May, the buds have bloomed.
May Day is the first Monday.

June, summer has begun.
June has the longest day of the year.

July, summertime holiday.
USA Independence Day.

August, the days are warm.
September, autumn begins.

October, Hallowe'en - the night ghosts are out.
Clocks go back.

November, USA Thanksgiving.
Saint Andrew's Day.

December, winter begins.
The shortest day of the year.
Christmas Day.

Chris Candeland (10)
Heswall County Primary School

CHILD'S THOUGHT

At eight, when I go to bed,
Wonderful things go through my head.
I think of animals in the wild,
Also small animals that are meek and mild.
I dream of fairies in the air,
With wands that shine and long fair hair.
I dream of lands that are far away,
I hope I can go there some sunny day.
I dream of wonderful golden fishes,
Which always give you magic wishes.

I dream of a horse with a very long mane,
And it's 6.15 so I catch the train.
I go to the zoo,
To see a lion and a kangaroo.
When it is time to go home,
I cry and start to moan.
So then I think of men with sharp swords,
Then I go to a hall with ladies and lords.
I think of rockets up in space,
Then they come down at a very fast pace.

In the morning when I wake again,
I bang my head and cry in pain.
All those thoughts ran out of my head,
'Time for breakfast' Mum said.

Gemma Wright
Heswall County Primary School

CALENDAR RHYME

January starts to fall with snow,
February winds start to blow.
In March we see new flowers,
And April comes with sunny showers.
In May the roses start to grow,
In June there is no snow.
July brightens up with the sun,
In August harvest has begun.
September turns, leaves are brown,
October makes leaves come down.
November brings the wind near,
December's here to end the year.

Tara Fairclough (10)
Heswall County Primary School

THE YEAR

January, falls the snow,
February comes very slow.
March starts to get sunny,
April, comes Easter Bunny.
May, the roses bloom so gay.
In June, July is on its way,
July the sun is bright,
August, there is lots of light,
September turns so very cold,
October, trees become old.
November, falls with rain,
December the year starts again.

Jayne Macdonald (9)
Heswall County Primary School

WEATHER

The weather is snowing,
>Snowing,
>>Snowing.

The weather is snowing,
>Snowing,
>>Snow.

My house is covered with ice,
>Ice,
>>Ice.

My house is covered with ice,
>Ice,
>>Ice.

I had a snowball fight,
>Fight,
>>Fight.

I had a snowball fight,
>Fight,
>>Fight.

I thought the weather was nice,
>Nice,
>>Nice.

I thought the weather was nice,
>Nice,
>>Nice.

My pet,
>Pet,
>>Pet,
>>>Pet , got very, very wet.

My dog,
            Dog,
                Dog,
                    Dog, ran through the fog.

Charlotte Parr (8)
Heswall County Primary School

A CHILD'S THOUGHT

At 9 o'clock I go to bed
Horrible pictures creep in my head.
Horrible noises go round and round,
Then suddenly there's no sound.
My brother snores loud in his bed,
He's so loud I can't rest my head.
I have lots of horrible dreams
But sometimes I dream of fishy streams.

They swirl around my little head,
At 9 when I go to bed.
At 6 o'clock I wake again,
The blood is pumping through my veins.
My mum is still quite fast asleep,
My dad's alarm clock goes *beep, beep.*
My daddy goes down all the stairs
The noises go away in pairs.

I get out of my warm, warm bed,
The pictures go out of my head.
My daddy goes out to the car
Then he drives very far.
At 9 o'clock I go to school
It is warm and very cool.

Kari Miles (9)
Heswall County Primary School

CALENDAR RHYME

January snow is all around.
February snow clears, now shoots are in the ground.
March the winds will blow
April showers come and go.
May new flowers are everywhere
June summer's in the air.
July ice-creams melt
August hot sun is felt.
September things are cooling down
October witches may come to town.
November fireworks light the sky
December Christmas spirits are high.

David Taylor (8)
Heswall County Primary School

A CHILD'S THOUGHT

At nine when I go to bed
football players are in my head.
They are running up the street
with a football at their feet.
Michael Owen, Robbie Fowler
people say he is a prowler.

Alan Shearer and Chris Sutton,
I noticed he lost a button.
Andy Cole and Ian Walker
I've been told he is a stalker.
Nigel Martyn and Steve Stone
he's so thin he's like a bone.

It's 7 o'clock and I'm awake
Mum's made cereal and I want cake.
I want football but it is school
I have to go it is the rule.
I'm in the car I'm on my way,
now I'm in school I want to play.

Christopher Greenhalgh (9)
Heswall County Primary School

TROUBLE AT THE FARM

Help! Help!
What is it now?
Zaffa the cat
Has lost his miaow!

Help! Help!
What do you need?
Billy the bull
Has done a bad deed!

Help! Help!
Now what's wrong?
Cathie the cow
Hit her head with a bang!

Help! Help!
What is the matter?
Pip the pig
Started talking latter!

At last the day is over
The muddles and troubles gone
I picked up a four-leaf clover
Thankful the day is done!

Alex Norton (9)
Heswall County Primary School

CALENDAR RHYME

January is very blowy,
February is very snowy.
March, the wildlife comes out,
April, the snowdrops dance about.
May, the sun peeps through the sky,
June, the swallows fly up high.
July, the sail boats sail on the sea,
August, I make sandcastles with Dad and Mummy.
September, I go up a year at school,
October, I go to the indoor swimming pool.
November, Santa wraps up the toys,
December, Santa gives them to the good girls and boys.

Stuart Brassey (8)
Heswall County Primary School

A CHILD'S THOUGHT

When I go to bed, I find a bird dead,
I think, am I dreaming in my bed?
A gentle blow, down and down the bird falls,
I cry out loud 'Help' but no one hears my calls.
I cry and cry till there's a puddle on the ground,
Then my mum says the bird has been found.

Now my dreams are happier, there's a smile on my face,
I just need to find a better place.
Somewhere by the sea or the River Dee,
With sand and boats and people to play with me.
I'm swimming in the sea with my friends from school,
And we hunt for crabs in the rock pool.

I go to school on a sunny day
I'd rather be out all day and play.
But in the afternoon it is our Christmas fair,
My mum says I can't go so I say 'I don't care.'
On Monday it is a baker day,
So all day Monday all I do is play.

Charlie Massegú Jones (9)
Heswall County Primary School

HELP!

Help! Help!
What to do?
Gip the gerbil
Is down the loo.

Help! Help!
What's the matter?
Daisy the cow
Has eaten the batter.

Help! Help!
What is that?
James the dog
Has eaten the cat.

Help! Help!
What is up?
My wife just
Squashed the duck.

Help! Help!
What's going on?
Oscar the pig
Has eaten the scone.

Richard Edmondson (9)
Heswall County Primary School

A CHILD'S THOUGHT

At eight when I go to bed
I find lovely pictures in my head,
From grizzly bears to picking flowers,
I dream I get some magic powers.
I wake up, it is morning,
I can hear my dad snoring.

I like to watch TV,
Especially CBBC.
I would like to be on Blue Peter,
Although Katy Hill could look much neater.
My favourite team is EFC
I would like to go out and see them play.

I watch Ready Steady Cook,
Then I read my school book.
Then finally I have my tea
And stroke my cat upon my knee.
And now again it's time for bed
I really want to rest my head.

Katie Owen (8)
Heswall County Primary School

WEATHER

The sun shines, shines,
It is lovely and hot.
The sea is shining,
And the crabs are warm.

The only trouble is,
You get sunburnt, burnt,
Then you have to put on sun cream.
You can have a picnic on the beach.

You can get fizzy drinks,
And have fish for your tea.
Sometimes the crabs,
Steal your lunch.

You can also buy ice-cream,
Which keeps you cool for the day.
You can lie on the sand,
And relax the whole day long.

Laura Parry (9)
Heswall County Primary School

CALENDAR RHYME

January brings the cold and animals are very bold.
February is getting warmer and there is a lot of trauma.
March brings the rain and it's February again.
April brings the showers with all the nice flowers.
May brings girls with all nice twirls in their hair.
June brings things like roses and fills people's hand with posies.
July brings the sun and is great fun.
August brings corn and harvest is born.
September brings lots and lots of fruit.
October brings all the ghosts and lots of spooks.
November brings lots of cold and all the leaves go gold.
December brings lots of sweets and nice treats.

Robert Williams (9)
Heswall County Primary School

THE CALENDAR POEM

January gets the snow,
February is wet and cold and gets the blow,
March is getting nearer to spring,
April the birds start to sing.
May the sheep start bleating,
June people keep on meeting.
July you get lots of sun,
August you get lots of fun.
September it starts to get cold,
October the leaves turn gold.
November the summer clothes are sold,
December the trees are old.

Graeme Matthews (9)
Heswall County Primary School

THE CALENDAR RHYME

January winds blow
February fires glow.
March blossom blooms,
April has no more dingy rooms,
May is end of spring,
June the birds sing.
July the summer is hot,
August the farmer farms his lot.
September animals go to sleep,
October cars go beep beep.
November fireworks hurt my ear
December is the end of the year.

Frances Harwood (9)
Heswall County Primary School

THE YEAR

January falls the snow,
February comes very slow.
March starts to get very funny,
April comes Easter Bunny.
May the roses bloom so gay,
In June, July is on its way,
July the sun is oh so bright,
August there is a lot of light.
September turns so very cold,
October trees become old.
November falls with lots of rain,
December, year starts again.

Ruth Fitzgerald (9)
Heswall County Primary School

MOTHER'S PIG

Mother's pig is very big,
He snorts around all day.
All he does is dig,
And always gets in the way.
Others think he is a nig,
Why do I stay
While he smells like a cig?
I think he should pay,
To stay and play with my wig.
But I never get a say,
In the future of this pig.

Michael Smith (11)
Kew Woods Primary School

WAR

War is the work of the Devil himself
Soldiers, kids and lots more lose their health.
And as if in slow-motion it begins to end
And you, yes you my friend
Could think only of the victory
Left behind researched in history.
Never would you think of wives waving
Kids all a-wailing
For their husband or their dad
Who might not return and some never had.
As they waved and cheered them on
Who would return, 50, 10 or none?
But as they died and withered away
Well my friend I have to say
Thought of victory
Left in history
Do you think God
Would give you the nod
On taking people's husbands, sons, dads or uncles
Away from these helpless souls?
And some of these very brave but dead soldiers
Are left still unknown
Over a piece of land
And now are buried in soil and sand.

Sarah McCabe (11)
Kew Woods Primary School

MY EYE-POPPING RECIPE

Now what shall I put in my recipe?
A juicy jellyfish from the sea,
A lizard and a bumblebee,
And the pips from the fruits of the apple tree.
I'll use thousands of other things as well,
My potion will have an awful smell!
I'll stir it short, I'll stir it long,
And hold your noses, it will pong!
I'll stir it 'til it's nice and thick
Just the thought of it makes me sick.
What would happen if I ate it?
Would it make me have a fit?
Would I go bang? Would I explode?
Would I go whizzing down the road?
Would I burp a cloud of smoke?
Or would I fizz like a can of Coke?
I wonder what it'd do to me?
Oh, well, here goes, let's wait and see . . .

Kayleigh Wiggins (11)
Kew Woods Primary School

TWISTER ALERT!

Twisters zoom round and round
Swing to the left
Swing to the right
Zoom forward
Zoom right back
Smashes everything in its path.

Emma Hopwood (9)
Kew Woods Primary School

THIS BEAR

This bear started off as a new fresh
piece of thread,
it was put on sale with a tag around its neck,
it was bought on a Tuesday.

This bear got dirty over the days and
has been soaked with bubbles from
the washing machine,
it has been dried in the tumble-dryer,
it has been hung by pegs on the line to dry.

This bear has been cuddled by many people,
it has had times when it's been thrown
on the floor, it's had rides around the
world in cars and aeroplanes.

This old bear is tattered and torn but it
is still loved,
it's been chewed on the ears by babies.

It has a lovely expression that's grown
over the years.

Emma Durkin (9)
Marshside Primary School

THIS CAR

This car has been down dark alleys,
it has crashed and had its windows smashed.
It has had five new bodies and has broken down too!

This car has been stuck in the sticky mud,
has been smacked, punched and kicked by thugs.
It has been fixed and looked at by mechanics.

This car has been filled up with diesel petrol,
it has been sat on and been wrecked.
Its rubber tyres have been punctured and popped.

This car is now crushed and smashed.
It has been replaced by another BMW car now,
and lies dead in the scrapyard.

Michael Hopson (8)
Marshside Primary School

THIS SHOE

This shoe has been lost many times,
its shoelaces are all tatty.
It has been walked in many times.

This shoe has been all over the big
house, it has been under beds,
in the kitchen and in the messy living room.

This shoe has been worn many times,
it has been worn by big boys,
and small girls.

This shoe has been chewed by fluffy dogs,
it has been in muddy puddles,
and it is smelly.

This shoe is white, red, purple,
it is an old shoe.

This shoe is dirty,
it has had a long life,
now it is ready to go in the dusty bin.

Laura Hunt (8)
Marshside Primary School

THIS SLIPPER

This slipper has been chewed by
dangerous dogs,
it has been lost many times,
this slipper has been found in the
rubbish bin.

This slipper is old,
it is smelly,
this slipper has had smelly feet in it.

This slipper has been on its own in the
dark night,
it has had all sorts of adventures,
it is all tatty now.

This slipper is in the bin and it will
never come out again,
it has had a good life,
it has had all sorts of accidents.

Coral Eastment (8)
Marshside Primary School

THIS CAR

This car has been up mountains, it has
crashed into the sea.
This car has been crushed, it has been up hills.

This car has been driven in the sun in
the morning, it has been in a garage and sat there.
This car has black tyres and it is red on the outside,
it had grey on the inside but now it is old.

This car has been ripped and torn,
it has been fixed by a mechanic.
This car has had a busy life.

Amy John (9)
Marshside Primary School

THIS FOOTBALL

This football has been taped up in a cardboard box in the attic,
and has been chewed by lots of different dogs,
and nearly been killed by cars.

This football has been kicked by lots of different people.
It has been signed on its hard leathery back by all
the Manchester United players,
and thrown back over the fence by the neighbours.

This football has been confiscated by my mum
because it has gone flying through house windows,
and Mr Wright has kept it in his room because it has
been lost in the cloakroom.
It has been flat and then been pumped back up by a ball pump.

This football has been on lots of different football pitches,
and hit people on their heads very hard.
It has been kicked through lots of muddy puddles.

This football has hit the crossbar many times and got hurt.
It has been sat on by people and changed into an oval shape.
It has bent people's fingers back and hurt people many times.

This football has been in the garden shed for a long time.
People have tried to pop it when they were mad.
It now lies in the garden, lonely on its own.

Matthew Whiteley (9)
Marshside Primary School

THIS SANDAL

This sandal has been bought by someone who loves it.
It has a home where people look after it.

This sandal has been chewed by bad babies.
It has been worn everywhere the person
who owns it goes.

This sandal has had lucky days and bad days.
It has been worn-out because of a big foot.
It has been to different countries.

This sandal has been scrubbed many times.
It has been wet and dirty with damp leaves on.
It has been to lots of sleepovers and
been dumped on the floor.

This sandal has been crushed, nobody
bothers with it anymore.
It is never to be seen again.

Alex Miller (9)
Marshside Primary School

THIS BED

This bed started off as brand new,
with a price tag on its long neck.
Soon someone bought it and they took it home.

This bed got a warm cover and a soft pillow,
soon messy children started to jump on it,
they hurt the neat poor bed.

This bed is getting smelly and tatty,
now people don't use it a lot.
It is up in the loft all alone with nobody to jump on it.

This bed, this useless bed is now on
the smelly and horrible junk pile,
it is all rotten, wet and cold.
This old and useless bed is very upset!

Emma Watts (9)
Marshside Primary School

THIS BOOK

This book has been put on dusty library shelves,
read lots of times,
it has been chewed by dangerous dogs.

This book has been scribbled on by naughty babies,
it has been sold at busy jumble sales
and read for night-time stories.

This book has told spooky stories,
it has been taken to junior school,
and been in lost property.

This book has been torn and tattered,
it has memories of when it was young,
and it is old now.

This book has ripped tatty pages,
it is now lonely in the empty attic,
it is never read at all.

Miriam Fullwood (9)
Marshside Primary School

THIS WATCH

This watch has been bought from a shop.
It has been wrapped up in paper,
and been tipped out of a stocking.

This watch has had its back taken off
with a screwdriver,
It has had its batteries taken out,
and has been broken many times.

This watch has been under water,
it has been in the swimming baths,
and been in a bubble bath.

This watch has a calculator on it,
and it has a loud alarm screech.

Ryan Brown (8)
Marshside Primary School

THIS SLIPPER

This slipper has been bought from a tiny shoe shop.
It is pink, inside it is fluffy and warm.

This slipper has been under my big bed,
it has been lost a few times,
and attacked by animals.

This slipper has been all around the huge house,
it has been walked in a lot,
and it is worn and battered.

This slipper has been new and now it is old.
It has happy memories,
and it doesn't fit me anymore.

Jessica Golder (9)
Marshside Primary School

MY LITTLE FRIEND

There's a hutch in my garden,
That stands there all year,
It seems very quiet,
Until I go near.

I have a look in,
What do I see?
A little nose twitching,
As fast as can be.

Then two pink eyes,
Looking at me,
She knows when I'm coming,
It's time to be fed.

Out on the garden,
She runs and hops,
My lovely white rabbit,
Her name is Snowdrop.

Claire Holroyd (9)
Oakdene County Primary School

I'M BIG AND SMALL

I'm big and small
But I never, never shrink
I'm as big as an elephant
And as small as a fish.
I can grow big and small
As big as a hall
But elephants and fishes
Don't grow at all.

Joanne Clark (9)
Oakdene County Primary School

LAZY

My sister is a chubby girl,
She sits upon her bed,
She's nothing else to do,
Except stare at Havakazoo.

My dad goes out to look at our zoo at the back of our house.
He feeds the tiger, the big black bear and stares at the stars.

My mum is helpful, she cooks and cleans,
She sometimes is very mean,
Lots of people aren't very well,
But she is sensitive like me.

Sally Rummery (10)
Oakdene County Primary School

FOOTBALL

F is for the FA Cup that you win every year,
O is for the offsides that are so close and near.
O is for the overhead kicks that you miss or score,
T is for the tight match when we lost five - four.
B is for bicycle kicks that you kick out of the air,
A is for Arsenal;, red and white is the colour they wear.
L is for linesmen that run up and down,
L is for the league, that you can be crowned.

Sean Moore (9)
Oakdene County Primary School

MY TOYS AREN'T ORDINARY TOYS

My toys aren't ordinary toys
My toys come alive at night
And make quite a lot of noise.
One night my teddy bears had a fight
It was a terrible fright for me
One teddy bear even lost his sight.
I didn't scream or shout or make as much noise as the teddy bears did
When they had a fight in the middle of the night.
My mum said I should be more interested in boys
Not my beloved mischief-making toys.

Helen MacDonald (10)
Oakdene County Primary School

MY DAD HE WAS A SCUBA-DIVER

My dad he was a scuba-diver
Then the world's best racing driver
Now he is a mountain ranger
Works all day in mortal danger.

My mum she was a good home-maker
Then she was a brilliant baker
Now she is a famous writer
And at night a kung fu fighter.

Amy Pritchard (10)
Oakdene County Primary School

MY BABY BROTHER

My baby brother,
To his toys he's like King Kong.
He throws his blocks around the house
because it makes a sound.

At mealtimes he's messy,
in fact all the time too.
It really makes me think,
that he belongs in the zoo!

Antonia McLoughlin (10)
Oakdene County Primary School

MY SISTER

Once my sister hit my hand,
I thought I'd broken my thumb,
My mother was not very pleased,.
And smacked her on the bum.

She cried all day and most of the night,
She really is a wimp,
I don't know what her problem is,
I only called her a chimp.

Jennifer Arnold (9)
Oakdene County Primary School

IN A POT

A dash of darkness from a blind man's eye,
A drop of fear from a piercing cry.
A touch of hate from an enemy's wish,
A pinch of sadness from a goodbye kiss.
            Deathly kiss, fearful wish.

A blob of death from a devil's thought,
Pot of trust from a judge's court.
A piece of glory from a deathly fight,
A portion of horror from a dying man's fright.
            Glorious fight, dead man's fright.

A sprinkling of gloom from a widow's heart,
A cup of jealousy for the better part.
A measure of joy from the heavenly sun,
A spoon of victory from a race soon won.
            Fiery sun, race soon won.

Jonathan Paul Kearns (11)
Our Lady's Junior School

WHAT IS . . . THE RAIN?

The rain is someone having a shower
in Heaven above.

It is someone watering the plants
in a neat, prim garden.

It is someone crying making puddles
here and there.

It is petals falling from a
white daisy.

Jenny Coughlin (10)
Our Lady's Junior School

NOVEMBER THE 5TH

November the 5th, a dark night like any other,
People waiting, waiting for amazing things to happen,
They wait for things called *fireworks.*

Fireworks are amazing things,
They whizz up in the air as if they have wings.
They explode like a bullet from a fearsome gun,
Like footballers when they have just won.
They have colours yellow, orange and white,
They fill the night with wonderful light.

They sound like bangs, crashes and crackles,
They also sound like witches' cackles.
They fill the world with sound and colour,
When they fade the world seems duller.
When Bonfire Night is here,
People say it's the best time of year.

Ashley Louise Evans (10)
Our Lady's Junior School

THE SECRET GARDEN

The entrance, the key
There is the life
A new beginning for Mary
A happy time.

The beautiful robin
Stood tall and proud
Cheeping and bobbing,
This is the way.

The wall stood tall
Like a guard of the garden
No one allowed
But Mary and robin.

Danielle Hughes (10)
Our Lady's Junior School

REMEMBER, REMEMBER THE 5TH OF NOVEMBER

Blazing fire in the moonlight
Dancing happily in the night.
Sparks flying up above
Gently floating like a dove.
Lighting up the dark, dark sky
Like a gymnast tumbling way up high.

Whistling continuously
Banging very briefly
Fireworks so loud they nearly scare me.

Catherine wheels spinning round
Sparks lying on the ground.
Lighting up a child's face
Hidden in this merry place.

The Catherine wheel like a ball
The people watching have it all.
Fireworks fly so high
When suddenly they say goodbye.

Sarah Lambe (10)
Our Lady's Junior School

WHAT IS THE MOON?

The moon is a giant lump of cheese
in the sky.

It is like a cookie in a never ending
cookie jar.

It is like a ball kicked up high
in the sky.

It is like an apple pie in
the oven.

It is like a doughnut floating in
the galaxy.

It is like a ball stuck up
a chimney.

Scott Pleavin (9)
Our Lady's Junior School

WHAT IS . . . THE SEA?

It is the sky
        that has fallen to the Earth.
It is a giant's cup
        full of water.
It is a blue sheet
        spread across the nations.
It is blue ink
        that a child has spilt.
It is a waterfall
        from heaven's golden gates.

Ross Couper (9)
Our Lady's Junior School

THE SECRET GARDEN

In this garden where I stare
With this lifeless garden bare
Will the robin show me the way
To a beautiful garden hidden away?

The stone-cold wall surrounds the place
With leaves and ivy in your face
The bushes and trees grow forever more
Covering the entrance to the hidden door.

I hope one day I find at last
The secret of its hidden past
When that day comes I'd like to share
The secrets that lie in there.

Danielle McGuinness (9)
Our Lady's Junior School

WHAT IS THE SAND?

Sand is yellow lines
On dark blue paper.
Sand is the yellow paper
In a bird's cage.
Sand is a giant's
Bowl of custard.
It is a big blanket of sunshine
That keeps you warm
It is golden water
Dripping through my hands.

Rebecca Price (10)
Our Lady's Junior School

A GARDEN OF LIFE

Walking through the garden,
Clearing a path,
Opening a new door,
A new door in Mary's heart.
It seemed like her garden,
For only she had the key,
To start a new beginning,
From something once dead,
A new place to escape,
A new place to find freedom,
Somewhere to explore,
Somewhere to love,
Once more.

Felicity Crease (11)
Our Lady's Junior School

WHAT IS THE SEA?

The sea is like a giant's
cup of water.
It is like a
soft blanket.
It is like a large
pool of ink.
It is like an
unravelled ball of silken thread.
It is like
a blue ribbon.

Rachael Kopanski (9)
Our Lady's Junior School

THE PLAYGROUND OF TIME

Swinging softly in the winter breeze
Always waiting for one lady's love
Seasons pass like never before
All those times are being reborn.

The chains turn to rust like thirsty ivy
The seat becomes cold like the wintry soil.

The wood cracks like an elderly face
And beneath the crack is a lovely child.

The garden again will come alive
Cracking the stone shell of a lonely heart
Giving birth to a brand-new start.

Michael Howard (10)
Our Lady's Junior School

MARY AND THE ROBIN

Mary went out to play,
She spotted a robin flying her way.
The robin flew right over her head,
Into the secret garden he fled.
Mary thought 'What's over there?'
Couldn't find a door anywhere.
Searching all over the place,
She found a door with a little key space.
Remembering the key she had found,
Put it in the key lock and turned it round.
Opening the creaky wooden door,
She stared at the garden she had never seen before.

Sophie Cassidy (10)
Our Lady's Junior School

WHAT IS . . . THE MOON?

The moon is a cookie
On a black plate.

It is a white elephant
Walking across the night sky.

It is a football being
Kicked about in space.

It is a plate
Floating across the sky.

It is a blob of white paint
On a piece of black card.

Ian Michael Kemp (11)
Our Lady's Junior School

THE ROBIN AND MARY

Mary saw a robin singing in a tree,
Come pretty robin, be a friend to me.
The robin took her to a door, hidden behind some
                                        ivy green,
The ivy grew so thick, the door could not be seen.
When Mary opened up the door
She found a garden neglected and bare,
All she could do was stand and stare.
The roses looked tangled, twisted and dead,
Nothing was growing, in the flower bed,
The robin sang sweetly, in the branches of the tree,
He seemed to sing a message especially for me.

Susie Ives (10)
Our Lady's Junior School

THE MOON

It is a silver coin
tossed up in the dark sky.

It is a piece of cheese
high in the sky.

It is God's lamp
glowing until morning arrives.

The moon is a long lamp post
guiding us from dangers.

The moon is a large ball of string
hanging from heaven.

Amanda Smith (10)
Our Lady's Junior School

THE EARTH

The Earth is a soft-ball
        hit into the air.

It is a blue dot
        on black paper.

It is the bluest part
        in a kaleidoscope.

It is a blue Tamagotchi
        in a Tamagotchi store.

It is a blue ball being
        juggled in a black tent.

Daniel Gunn (9)
Our Lady's Junior School

CLOUDS

The clouds are like balls of wool
Floating in the air.

They are like a lump of candyfloss
Taken from a child.

They are like white beanbags
Swaying in the sky.

They are like bubbles
On top of a sink.

They are like a big white meringue
Ready for someone to eat.

Katie Hulley (10)
Our Lady's Junior School

WHAT IS THE . . . FROST?

The frost is like a tiny star,
                    falling from the sky.

It is the sparkles from a Christmas tree
                    shining in the light.

It is the coating of icing sugar
                    sprinkled all around.

It is a sheet of white paper
                    spread along the ground.

It is the sparkles from the sparklers
                    shining in the night.

Jade Sliwka (10)
Our Lady's Junior School

WHAT IS A STAR?

A star is our dead relative
Watching over us.

A star is an angel's glow
Stopping for the night.

A star is a Frisbee
Lost in the sky.

A star is a diamond
Shining in the night.

A star is a drop of milk
On a great black surface.

Christopher Holmes (11)
Our Lady's Junior School

OUR KITTENS

We have just bought two new kittens,
Their names are Dillon and Floss,
My mum and dad got bitten,
And both were very cross!

When I go to sleep each evening,
They come into my bed.
They stop me from going straight to sleep,
So I play with them instead.

They scratch the chair and curtains,
And sometimes make a mess,
But I love my two new kittens,
They are the very best!

Bethany Wilson (8)
Our Lady of Lourdes RC Primary School

WITHOUT YOU GOD

Without you God
people wouldn't have a world to
live on.
Without you God
people wouldn't know where to get
their ketchup from!
Without you God
I wouldn't live.
Without you God
there would be no love
to give.
Without you God
the world would end.
Without you God
there would be no money
to spend.
Without you God
we would have
no sport.
Without you God
there would be no
pigs that snort.
Without you God
the sun wouldn't
exist.
Without you God
there would be
no weather, not even
mist.
Without you God
there would be no
light.

Without you God
we would have
no sight.
Put it this way,
without you God
not a thing would be here.

Michael Taylor (7)
Our Lady of Lourdes RC Primary School

THE KEY

The shimmering key unlatches,
The ancient rotted door,
Creaking as it opens,
Slowly opening,
And there it was.
Lying there still, as still as a house,
As still as a bone buried underground,
As still as the wind on a hot, hot summer's day.
There it was,
                    Gold.

Estelle Smith (11)
Our Lady of Lourdes RC Primary School

GREEN

Green is a dewdrop in spring.
Green is a field in early morning.
Green is the freshness of a waterfall.
Green is a shining emerald.
Green is the dawning of a new day.

Natasha Oakley (9)
Our Lady of Lourdes RC Primary School

RED

Red is a sunset glowing bright
Red is blood on a razor-sharp dagger,
Red is a fire with anger and might,
Red are roses in a crystal-cut vase.

Rachael Little (10)
Our Lady of Lourdes RC Primary School

KEYS

Shiny keys turn,
Attached to sparkling key-rings.
Jagged teeth bite the lock,
The rusty door opens.

Jennifer Connaughton (12)
Our Lady of Lourdes RC Primary School

HAILSTONE

Hailstone crystals swoop down mountains,
And crack like thin glass,
Breaking into tiny diamonds.

Jamie Norris (11)
Our Lady of Lourdes RC Primary School

SPIDER WEBS TWINKLE

Spider webs twinkle
In the fresh winter air,
Like fragments of shining glass.

Kate Stevens (11)
Our Lady of Lourdes RC Primary School

AN EMPTY CAN

A dripping, empty can,
Flung on the pavement,
Rolling in the street,
Resting beside a deserted postbox.

Corinne Mellor (11)
Our Lady of Lourdes RC Primary School

LIGHT BLUE

The sky free from clouds.
Dolphins diving in the calm sea.
Blue tits chirping from the trees.
Ice melting to nothing.

Danielle Howard (9)
Our Lady of Lourdes RC Primary School

THE KEY

Ancient key unlocks
The creaking door
Disturbing the angry gods!

Christopher Thomson (11)
Our Lady of Lourdes RC Primary School

STARS

Stars align the cold night sky,
Twinkling like gold from a baking mine,
Each one an individual god to its own world.

Roua McHugh (11)
Our Lady of Lourdes RC Primary School

MY RABBIT LISTER

We love our rabbit Lister
He is so cute and small
But when he looks up at us he thinks
We must be tall.

He is a little menace so we
Keep him in a hutch
But when he's out
He runs about
We love him very much.

Karl Hansen (8)
Our Lady of Lourdes RC Primary School

GOLD

The stars glistening in the sky,
Happiness growing through the land,
Love is singing throughout the world,
People cheering as the Premier League Cup is lifted.
Clouds showing the wind the way to blow.

Stacey Rodwell (9)
Our Lady of Lourdes RC Primary School

THE SEA IS DARK BLUE

The storm, rain is falling,
Dark blue is the colour of the sea,
Ships crashing into rocks,
The waves taking no prisoners,
Sailors beware, sailors beware!

Tom Ibison (10)
Our Lady of Lourdes RC Primary School

MOONLIGHT

Still as can be, the moon glinted in the sky.
Everything was a mysterious silver colour.
Dewdrops on the grass,
As the stars shone like diamonds in the sky.
It was a dazzling sight.
Everything was an amazing silver.
I stood and stared,
As the wind blew through the trees.
Everything had a shadow, as black as can be.

Vicki Winstanley (9)
Our Lady of Lourdes RC Primary School

RED

Red is Hell burning and burning,
Red is the Devil laughing and laughing,
Red is lava flowing down a volcano,
Red is a fire sizzling out loud,
Red is blood on the carving knife!

Martin Thompson (9)
Our Lady of Lourdes RC Primary School

BLACK

Black is hurtling into space,
Black is being surrounded in silence,
Black is a dagger raised to stab,
Black is the scream of someone dying,
Black is falling . . . ever falling.

Sophie Jagger (9)
Our Lady of Lourdes RC Primary School

SPRING

Once a year spring comes around
Fields and meadows covered in fairgrounds
Country fairs and Ferris wheels,
Car-boot sales and lots of deals.

People walking, people talking
People hearing pigeons squawking,
Spring lambs jump for joy
While babies shout and scream for toys.

Jennifer Cox (10)
Our Lady of Lourdes RC Primary School

SPRING

A rare
daffodil,
grows in the
dusty border
of the empty
road.

Charlotte Molyneux (11)
Our Lady of Lourdes RC Primary School

CINQUAIN

Wolves
Rapidly chasing,
Gaining on you,
Angrily pursuing closer, closer . . .
Safe!

David Flynn (11)
Our Lady of Lourdes RC Primary School

OUT OF ASSEMBLY!

Mr Train's class *choo-chooed* out of assembly,
Mr Storm's class *thundered* out of assembly,
Mr Duke's class *marched* out of assembly,
Mr Slow's class *strolled* out of assembly,
Mr Sport's class *raced* out of assembly,
Mr Rocket's class *launched* out of assembly,
Miss Ice's class *skated* out of assembly,
Miss Quiet's class *tiptoed* out of assembly.

Emilia Grilli (11)
Our Lady of Lourdes RC Primary School

BLUE

The sky with its soft fluffy clouds,
A fresh day cold and windy,
Blue is water flowing down the stream,
A bluebell and other kinds of flowers,
Blue makes me happy and glad,
Blue takes me away into a world of my own.

Nicola Stone (10)
Our Lady of Lourdes RC Primary School

SPRING

Cracking eggs
hatching,
Fluffy newborn
chicks pop out,
Under mother's
wings.

Elizabeth Harris (11)
Our Lady of Lourdes RC Primary School

SPRINGTIME

In springtime . . .
>fluffy chicks hatch,
>white lambs struggle,
>racing rabbits hop,
>joyful birds twitter,
>twisting tadpoles stretch,
>jumping frogs gulp,
>>. . . new life begins.

Dean Reilly (11)
Our Lady of Lourdes RC Primary School

OUT OF ASSEMBLY

Miss Bolton's class *bolted* out of assembly.
Mr Ward's class was *stretchered* out of assembly.
Mrs Jackson's class *sang* out of assembly.
Miss Hird's class *stampeded* out of assembly.
Mrs Bridge's class *collapsed* during assembly.
Mrs Fyle's class *organised* their way out of assembly!

Rebecca Holmes (11)
Our Lady of Lourdes RC Primary School

THE MINIBEAST JUNGLE

In the long grass at the bottom of my garden
I found . . .
>a busy bumble bee buzzing,
>a wiggly worm wandering,
>a moaning moth mumbling,
>>. . . a minibeast jungle!

Sean Ibison (7)
Our Lady of Lourdes RC Primary School

SPRING

Spring weather
comes,
Grey clouds
disappear,
Winter rain
wanders,
God's heavens open,
Spring sun shines.

Holly Kirby (11)
Our Lady of Lourdes RC Primary School

MOONLIGHT

Moonlight shines in the lake,
Reflections of the trees.
The moon shines like a crystal in the sky.
The stars light up in the sky.
The fish reflect in the water.
The rocks shine like stars.

Nathan Radford (9)
Our Lady of Lourdes RC Primary School

THE MINIBEAST JUNGLE

In the long grass at the bottom of my garden
I found . . .
a small slug slithering,
a hairy spider crawling,
a fluffy moth flying,
. . . a minibeast jungle!

Laurence Cox (6)
Our Lady of Lourdes RC Primary School

MOONLIGHT

Children sleep while the moonlight
                               dazzles on them.
Wolves howl in the moonlight.
Silver stars twinkle in the dark blue sky.
The river is shimmering.
Stones shine like crystals.
Owls *tu-whit tu-whoo* in dark, hollow trees,
But I am going to *s l e e p* . . .

Sarah Weir (9)
Our Lady of Lourdes RC Primary School

MOONLIGHT

The moon glimmers at dead of night.
The snap of a twig could give you a fright.
Garden silver, silver as can be.
Ponds are sparkling brightly as can be,
Stars are shining like crystal
And after moon-fall, night frightens me.

Sam Bryce (9)
Our Lady of Lourdes RC Primary School

MOONLIGHT

The twinkling of the stars,
Moonlight turning everything it touches to silver,
A silver ocean,
Sparkling spider webs,
With sparkling silver threads,
Surround the coconut spider's territory.

Matthew Todd (8)
Our Lady of Lourdes RC Primary School

MOONLIGHT

The pitch-black sky glistens with silver.
Stars glisten as the dazzling moon shines on all the land.
Not even a mouse can be heard.
Crystal-like grass shimmers,
Owls' eyes twinkle in the darkness.
The shimmering leaves rustle on trees.
Total silence throughout the land.

Will Wright (8)
Our Lady of Lourdes RC Primary School

MOONLIGHT

The moonlit sky is like black velvet.
The spider's web in the corner of the garden, glistening like silver.
The stars are like silver buttons shining brightly.
The pond is shimmering in the moonlight.
The moon shines on the grass,
Not a whistle of wind,
Just harmony, not a sound to be heard.

Callum Gregson (9)
Our Lady of Lourdes RC Primary School

MOONLIGHT

The stars in the deep blue sky glimmer as if
they are diamonds.
Everything is quiet and the river is
Shimmering in the moonlight shadow.
The sand is moving from side to side
With a short and quick breeze of the wind.

Natalie Lockhart (9)
Our Lady of Lourdes RC Primary School

MINIBEAST JUNGLE

At the bottom of my garden, in the long grass,
I found . . .
> a busy bumble bee humming,
> a slippery worm falling,
> a tropical beetle crawling,
> a creeping spider spinning,
> > . . . a minibeast jungle!

Katrina Casterton (7)
Our Lady of Lourdes RC Primary School

THE MINIBEAST JUNGLE

In the long grass at the bottom of my garden
I found . . .
> a green grasshopper bouncing,
> a beautiful butterfly flying,
> a busy bumble bee buzzing,
> a slow snail sliding,
> > . . . a minibeast jungle!

Rosie Burke (7)
Our Lady of Lourdes RC Primary School

FOOTBALL BOOTS

Crumbled soles break like bread,
Floppy tongues droop,
Worn studs chipped like stone,
Stringy laces loop.
Rough leather is worn,
Dirty boots sprint, like the wind,
Old boots are torn.

Philip Cook (11)
Our Lady of Lourdes RC Primary School

FROZEN PUDDLES

Frozen puddles lying peacefully,
Hailstones shoot down like thunderbolts,
Shattering the ice.
No more tranquil puddles.

Carly West (11)
Our Lady of Lourdes RC Primary School

ORANGE

Orange is a vase of glowing marigolds,
Orange is a jar of marmalade sitting in a cupboard,
Orange is the hair of a gerbil,
Orange is a tangerine in a little bowl.

Rachel Simpson (9)
Our Lady of Lourdes RC Primary School

BLACK

Black is a sign of evil and war,
Black is a plain picture of darkness,
Space is black and silent, like an open field.

James Bridge (10)
Our Lady of Lourdes RC Primary School

SNOW

Cold snow drifting down,
Like pieces of torn paper,
Falling to the ground.

Ben Sharples (11)
Our Lady of Lourdes RC Primary School

THE MINIBEAST JUNGLE

At the bottom of my garden in the tall grass
I found . . .
       a striped tree-hopper springing,
       a slippery worm slithering,
       a spotted ladybird creeping,
       a noisy grasshopper bouncing,
            . . . a minibeast jungle!

Jenny Barton (7)
Our Lady of Lourdes RC Primary School

SPRINGTIME

In springtime . . .
       cuddly chicks chirp,
       smiling squirrels stumble,
       tiny tadpoles twirl,
       baby birds bounce,
       handsome hedgehogs huddle
           new life everywhere.

Leanne Conway (10)
Our Lady of Lourdes RC Primary School

COSMIC

C ounting planets, stars and all,
O h! what a beautiful place.
S tars are gleaming in the sky,
M ars, Jupiter, Pluto and Saturn
I n, out, all around they move,
C osmic's world, cosmic's land.

Eleanor Hopkins (10)
Rainford CE Primary School

ALIEN RACE!

I went up into space and saw a face
It was the face at the start of an alien race
I looked around and what I found
Were goggly eyes all bouncing round
Spots were prancing
Feet were dancing
The whistle went *pheeww!*
And the aliens flew
Colours went whizzing
Green, black and blue
Fat ones
Thin ones
Big ones
Little ones
Grimy ones
Slimy ones
And even a baldy one
I watched the fun
To see who had won
My heart filled with dread
When I saw the bald head
And I saw the alien face
Who won the alien race
But then I felt glad
When I saw it was . . . my dad!

Mandy McBlain (10)
Rainford CE Primary School

COSMIC

One night I had a dream,
But it was not about ice-cream.
It was about an alien scene.

I flew to Mars past the stars,
And past the Milky Way,
When I saw the sights the stars so bright,
I knew I had to stay.

When there in the distance,
I saw something green,
It looked like an alien,
So I hid behind a crater,
And looked a little later,
To see if he had gone.

But then I woke up,
Tit, tut, tut,
I had had a wonderful time,
So I wrote this poem about cosmic,
And made sure it rhymed.

So there you have it a cosmic scene,
In a dream with me,
Mars and the stars and the Milky Way.
The next time I go I've got to stay.

Laura Brennan (10)
Rainford CE Primary School

COSMIC

I was flying through the cosmos
Searching for a crazy cosmic world.
Shining stars turned to supernovas in this super-sized world.
Crazy green lean creatures cowering in craters
As I zoomed past at light speed looking for a crazy cosmic world.
My super spaceship sped past the crazy cosmic constellations
In search of a crazy cosmic world,
A big black hole appeared and sucked in my super spaceship
And inside was my crazy cosmic world,
Where planets were pyramids and tasted like pineapple
And stars looked like silver shining sultanas
And massive cratered moons tasted of mint.
On the planet Zag where aliens play tag,
I joined a planet feast where we ate the planet.
I went to planet Kyne where the beasts always whine.
Oh no! It's dinnertime and I can't get out!

Tom Latham (10)
Rainford CE Primary School

COSMIC

I happened to be flying through space,
When all of a sudden in my face,
In walked a spaceman,
Who on his head he wore a pan,
'Hello,' he said, and I said, 'Hi.'
'Shall I teach you how to fly?'
'I know,' I said.
'Take that pan off your head.'
'Let's be best friends to stay.'
'Come on let's fly to the Milky Way.'

Roxanne Gore (10)
Rainford CE Primary School

COSMIC

I went to space
And there I was standing face to face
With an alien from outer space.
He said, *'Gobble goo.'*
I said, 'How are you?'
He said, *'De be re de.'*
I said, 'Come with me.'
He said, *'Gobble goo glame.'*
I said, 'Is that your name?'
He said, *'I bere plot.'*
I said, 'Sorry, what?'
He said, *'E berry ammy.'*
I said, 'Got a family?'
He said, *'Goberry deet deet.'*
I said, Want a sweet?'
I said, 'Sorry I do not understand.'
He said, 'You humans are useless.'

Danielle Simone Robinson (10)
Rainford CE Primary School

COSMIC

There was a young lady called Grace,
Who decided to fly up to space,
So she bought some supplies,
And said her goodbyes,
Then shot up to that unusual place.

She was flying around like a bird,
Without a care in the world,
Till the engine cut out,
And she gave a loud shout,
But none of the *aliens* cared.

She was whizzing down through space,
At a tremendous pace,
Till she hit the ground,
With a terrible pound,
And said, *'What a disastrous place.'*

Richard Makin (10)
Rainford CE Primary School

COSMIC

In the distant future,
A man named Cosmic
Jumped into his spaceship,
Ready to find a new world.
This man was no ordinary man,
He was a man from another world.

His skin is purple,
And his language is weird,
He only has one eye as well.

As his spaceship points up to space,
He listens out for, *'Cleared for take-off.'*
Then he hears it,
And *blast!*

As he is now in outer space,
Ready to find a new world,
He sees something in the distance,
A planet?
Another world?
Yes it is,
And he calls it *Cosmic!*

Daniel Smith (9)
Rainford CE Primary School

COSMIC

I was on my way to Mars,
And I saw lots and lots of stars,
Some were red, some were green,
Some were blue and yellow too.
I whooshed past them like a dart.
Suddenly, *crash!*
I got out of my spaceship,
I had a look around.
Then I heard, 'Gobble, gobble.'
An ugly thing stuck its head from behind a mound,
It was ugly and disgusting but very small.
He looked like a baby but no, not at all.
He asked me if I'd like to stay for tea,
I said, 'Yes please. I am quite hungry.'
I wonder what I'm having for tea?

Laura Preston (10)
Rainford CE Primary School

COSMIC

Aliens and spaceships are what I can see
Planets and stars there would be.
Some planets are big, some are small
But my favourite one would be quite tall.
There in the distance I saw something green
It was glowing with a big bright beam
It came closer and closer with two big eyes
I was looking for a place to hide
I shivered with fear
As it came quite near
Then it disappeared.

Joanna Kiddy (10)
Rainford CE Primary School

COSMIC

I flew into space at a very fast pace,
I whizzed past Mars and stars and chocolate bars,
A thousand stars lit up the sky,
With nebulae lying all over
Space is such a wonderful place
Nearer to Earth than Pluto
But not close to anywhere
For space is situated smack, bang
Right in the middle of nowhere.
Scientists say we're not alone
We are alone.
I've been to space there's nothing there
Except perhaps a few planets and stars.

Philip Whitby (10)
Rainford CE Primary School

COSMIC!

I went into space
What a strange place
Now you come to think of it
Green, fluffy monsters
Saucers bright pink
Big long noses
Mind you I would like to
meet them!
Yet I wonder what they're
really like.
Hmm! Pop!

Rachel Large (10)
Rainford CE Primary School

COSMIC

5, make your will,
4, say your prayers,
3, press the ignition,
2, rise into the air,
1, blast into space,
At such a tremendous speed,
Whiz around the universe
At supersonic speed.

Past Mercury, Saturn,
Pluto and Mars
See all the planets
And all the stars.

Andrew Lyon (10)
Rainford CE Primary School

COSMIC

There's many things that I have seen
And many places that I have been.
I've seen moons and stars,
I want to see Pluto and Mars
But I really want to see cars.
I'm in space,
It's a quiet place.
I'm free, free as a bird
But there's one thing that I've not heard,
Been, or even seen.
That's cosmic!

David Stove (10)
Rainford CE Primary School

COSMIC

I went up to space
To see the cosmic place
In a rocket
Here I go to the galaxy
All the way
Stars are bright
It's really quite a sight
The aliens are green
And not very clean
But as long as I am a human
I will survive.

Christopher Critchley (10)
Rainford CE Primary School

MONEY

I'm in my bedroom
     and looking around
For lots of money
     that will make a pound
I go to the shop
     to buy a ticket
I get lots of luck
     from a friendly cricket
I turn on the TV
     to watch the draw
All six balls
     who could ask for more!
I feel rather funny
     as I collect the money
All I have to do is spend,
     that is a happy end!

Catherine Brady (9)
St Alban's RC School, Wirral

COSMIC!

Oh there's the moon,
The colour of a spoon.
The glistening sun,
In the shape of a bun,
Yes it's definitely Cosmic!

The roaring of a rocket,
In the shape of my pocket.
The revolving moon,
Will be going soon,
Yes it's definitely Cosmic!

The shining stars,
Like bright-coloured cars.
Outer space,
What a massive place,
Yes it's definitely Cosmic!

Oh space is so lonely,
To be the only
Person in miles and miles,
Certainly raises no smiles.
Perhaps it's not so Cosmic after all.

But still Cosmic is a wonderful word,
As you have probably heard,
I love it!

Rachael Clay (11)
St Alban's RC School, Wirral

THE RAGING SUN

There was a sun called the raging sun
It charges up when night has gone
It charges across the sky all day
But when night comes it goes away.

Marcus Smith (9)
St Alban's RC School, Wirral

THE CONCERT

The music at the concert goes boom, boom, boom
As loud as a big base drum through a microphone.
Kisses, hugs and autographs,
Posters are the best part of the concert.

Katie Melling (8)
St Alban's RC School, Wirral

DAYLIGHT TO NIGHT LIGHT

Daylight is hot because of the burning sun
But when it settles down the night light comes
Once again everybody lays their heads
But then the sun comes again.

Matthew Wilson (9)
St Alban's RC School, Wirral

A STORMY NIGHT

In the town it's teeming
People are screaming, 'My washing'
People scuttle, children mutter
How silly grown-ups are.

Jenny Meyers (8)
St Alban's RC School, Wirral

UNTITLED

Thunder rumbled, lightning flashed.
Hailstones fell, rain lashed.
Wind rushed through the woods
And leaves falling to the ground.

Sarah Lowndes (8)
St Alban's RC School, Wirral

A STORMY NIGHT

One dark stormy night
The wind is blowing hard
All we can hear is rainfall
And the wind blowing.

Michelle White (9)
St Alban's RC School, Wirral

COSMIC!

It's a cosmic world,
Planets spinning
Rockets blasting
Shooting rocks
Starlit space, silence!

The Earth
Revolving around
The blazing sun
The source of life
For everyone.

The moon
Mirrors the sun
At night
Helping our cosmic sight.

Pluto
Is a little place
It's very dry and very cold
It's the furthest from the pot of gold.

The burning gold of the sun
Is the source of the light
It keeps my world ever so bright.

Sara Lynch (11)
St Alban's RC School, Wirral

A STORMY NIGHT

The wind squeals and whistles
The lightning goes crash, the thunder rolls
The wind screeches
And all the trees clatter.

Christina O'Brien (9)
St Alban's RC School, Wirral

COSMIC!

Water flowing on the moon,
How it would be fun.
Swimming around in a spacious lagoon,
Swimming towards the sun!

Alien life forms,
An alien place.
Life would be exciting,
In outer space!

Floating around
Over never-ending space.
There is no ground,
No landing place!

No need to be alone,
No need to fear,
As my friends and family
Could be near!

As on the moon
Water may flow,
My friends and family
We would all go!

Lisa Fadden (11)
St Alban's RC School, Wirral

THE MOON

The silk of the moon will come out soon
To shine the light in the black night sky.

The moon follows when we drive around,
The moon is gone when we turn around.

Joe Carroll (9)
St Alban's RC School, Wirral

REAL MONSTERS!

The creeping of the floorboards
The way the monster growls
It is so very scary
When the monster howls.
If that doesn't scare you
I don't know what will,
The only thing to save you
Is to go for
And kill!
You hunt that scary monster
And trace his every step,
But watch out for those fang teeth
They'll trap you like a net.
You will never catch him
Even if you try
For he's more clever,
Beware and never, ever
Try and be more clever
For you'll never, ever
Ever be more clever
Than the monster's growl!

Joe Catterall (9)
St Alban's RC School, Wirral

CRASHING THUNDER AT NIGHT

One night when I was in bed,
I heard the thunder twirling around in my head
It crashed bumped and twirled all around
All the trees crashed. Oh my window!
Oh no! The window smashed
The next night was the same.

Victoria Killen (8)
St Alban's RC School, Wirral

COSMIC

Out in space it's an eerie place,
Loads of stars and planets.
The sun is shining,
Making everything starlit.
There is the Earth slowly revolving round the sun.

Whoosh! goes a shooting star,
Spinning, spinning goes the moon,
All the stars looking like shapes,
So beautiful and silent.
Then it isn't for long,
I see a rocket slowly blasting off.

The planets are all multicoloured,
Red, blue, yellow and green,
Some hot, some cold,
That's what I've been told.
Big craters on the moon,
Deep and dull, no colour at all,
With grey and blacks,
I would love to go back.

Daniel Lawrence (11)
St Alban's RC School, Wirral

SPAGHETTI

Spaghetti, spaghetti everywhere
on your face and in your hair.
But I like it best in my mouth
Slippy, slidey and roundabout.
It slides down slow to my tum
It's then I know that I am full.

Martin Clarke (8)
St Alban's RC School, Wirral

COSMIC!

Space is black, as black can be,
With lots to explore for you and me.
A starry tunnel, silent but clear,
We fly through space with endless fear.

But wouldn't it be *Cosmic!*

Stars of silver all around,
We float through space, but still no sound.
Empty space there's nothing to see,
But I would really love to be
An astronaut from out of space,
Flying through the air in a wonderful place.

Wouldn't it be *Cosmic!*

Comets flying here and there,
If you get hit you'll have a scare.
As for the sun, a ball of fire,
Go too near and you'll expire.

But wouldn't it be *Cosmic!*

Holly Byrne (11)
St Alban's RC School, Wirral

THE SUN SONG

The sun winks as the day goes by
Birds flying past the sky.
When it comes to sunset
The sun sings us a lullaby.
Sweet and soft it drifts by
through the night sky.

Samantha Schorah (8)
St Alban's RC School, Wirral

COSMIC

Dark, scary and frightening too,
The magic is all around you!
The sun, the moon and the stars,
And the deep red of out-of-space Mars.

Twisting and turning,
Bright colours are burning.
Yellows, purples and luminous green,
Completely and everywhere to be seen.

Mysterious, wonderful and amazing,
All around you is changing,
The power of a blast,
It shoots so fast.

A wonderful feeling,
All that magical dreaming.
Leading the way,
Each and every day,
It's all one meaning . . .
                    Cosmic!

Laura Greene (11)
St Alban's RC School, Wirral

BOWLING

I choose my ball,
My fingers fit,
It feels just right for me,
I look down the lane,
I take my aim,
And I hope I win this game.

Peter Sprott (9)
St Alban's RC School, Wirral

COSMIC

Outer space
A futuristic frontier
A black and distant tunnel
Too far to see through
Like a dark
Pitch-black passage
Lit by stars
Space's innocent candles
A never-ending black curtain
Doesn't know when to stop
And reveal the edge of discovery
It clasps and holds in its grip
Planets
Civilisations
Suns
Cosmic dust
If the black curtain ever opened
Where would it stop and unearth what lies beyond
Cosmic space.

Jacinta Warwick (10)
St Alban's RC School, Wirral

COSMIC

Up in space it's a dark black place,
Where the stars are shining
brightly in the velvet sky,
The shooting stars sweep across the sky,
As I see them going by,
I see the planets travelling round and round,
They're a long long way from the ground.

Hannah McMahon (11)
St Alban's RC School, Wirral

SEASONS

I watch the seasons pass me by
With time they change like the colour of the sky,
In summer it's blue, not a cloud in sight,
In winter it's cloudy and dark like the night.
I love the sun so warm and bright,
The thought of ice-cream fills me with delight.
Along comes autumn the leaves start to fall,
The ground is covered in red, yellow and brown
As the leaves keep tumbling down,
Next comes winter all icy with snow,
I sit by the fire, my face all aglow,
Out comes my scarf, hat and gloves,
To keep warm I make sure of that.
The snowflakes glisten, everywhere is white,
Most of the animals hibernate, not one in sight,
Spring is the best as the buds appear,
The sky gets bluer and starts to clear,
This is why spring is the best.

Karlee Louise Daniels (9)
St Alban's RC School, Wirral

THE MOON

I'm riding along in my spaceship
        for all the world to see,
I've left the world behind me now,
        what's in front of me?
The moon flies by, the planets spin,
        speeding past the moon
It's the moon I want to land on
        I wonder what happens up there?

Claire Donnelly (9)
St Alban's RC School, Wirral

COSMIC

The stars so bright
The night is right
Shooting stars so cosmic
And it reminds me of a comet.

The shooting stars have gone in
Now they're shining like tin,
The planets stars I mean
But not the shooting stars that I've just seen.

We look from Earth
Even if you live in Perth,
The cosmic light
Is so brightly bright,
The cosmic light goes round the universe
Like a small song verse,
When it comes here it looks like a comet
But it is so cosmic.

Craig Ward (11)
St Alban's RC School, Wirral

THE SUMMER BIRDS

The summer birds have come and gone
And in the early winter sun
A soft and sweet sparrow pecks the frozen ground
But
        Stops to listen
           for
         the worms'
          wriggly
            round

Kathryn McMinn (8)
St Alban's RC School, Wirral

COSMIC!

Out in space everything flies
You look at a rocket passing by
Watching the stars
And glancing at Mars.
The moon is bright
Sparkling at night.

All the planets big and small
(Back down there you see nothing at all.)
All is dark and silent too
A couple of planets, a lovely view.

Up in the sky it's a very big place
I see a man floating in space.
Everything I see is big and round
Up in space there's not a sound.

Nadia Lloyd (10)
St Alban's RC School, Wirral

COSMIC!

Space, it's big, long and bright
It goes on all day and night
You feel weightless as air
In space no one is there
And I wonder?
It's an unexplained and a deserted place
It's dark and creepy up in space
I watch the sun rise and set in the sky
And I wonder why.

Heather M'Ardle (11)
St Alban's RC School, Wirral

COSMIC

Space is dark
With twinkling lights,
There is a star
Which is called the sun
Which is big and fat,
Like a sticky iced bun.
But there is a place
Which is really ace.
It's called Venus.

There's shining stars
All around Mars.
Floating around in space
Not a care,
Apart from that I forgot my suitcase.

Jayne Neill (11)
St Alban's RC School, Wirral

BIRDS

If all the birds up in the sky
Stopped singing for one minute
Then one by one start up again
The hawk, the thrush, the linnet
The sound it would be deafening
Upon the ears so harsh
Circling as they gathered
Flying low across the marsh.
The monarch of the water,
The swan so white, so regal
Guardian of her cygnets
Her eyes upon the watching eagle.

D Saville (9)
St Alban's RC School, Wirral

COSMIC

Darkness all but one star
Strange as anything, black as tar,
Continuously revolving around a star so bright
Which feeds the planets their only light.

Comets whizzing, planets revolving
So silent as if no mystery needs solving
It's as if you are spinning and the planets stay still,
And black holes turning ready to kill.

Unlike Earth there's no oxygen in space
Another planet is a lonely place.
For in space you feel light as air
And ever so lonely, for no one is there.

Luke Marsden-Rafferty (11)
St Alban's RC School, Wirral

COSMIC

Dark and silent, you're all alone,
No one to talk to and you can't go home.
There's twinkly lights and it's always night,
Earth cannot be seen, it's just you and your tin of baked beans.
Shooting stars go by in the dark and misty sky,
Out here I will die away from all my family
and in the dark and misty sky.

Floating high, high, high into the misty sky
I'm travelling fast it's probably my last.
I'm very cold but I must have been bold,
Here comes my last breath I am very near my slow
and painless death.

Patrick Carroll (11)
St Alban's RC School, Wirral

STORMY DAY

The thunder *booms* and echoes loudly.
The lightning *crackles* and flashes brightly.
The trees bend and *crack* and creak.
The wind *blows* and whistles loudly.
The leaves scramble and *crunch* nosily.
The people push through the *blowing* wind.
The foxes *sprint* to their burrows.
The wind gets louder, the thunder *booms.*
The lightning *flashes* the trees crash,
The leaves scramble, the foxes sprint
And the people shout.
'There's a storm a-blowing!'
'There's a storm a-blowing!'

Anthony Woodward (9)
St Alban's RC School, Wirral

TWO MEN ON A BEACH

There were two men named Jake and Scott,
They sailed away in a pale blue yacht.
They sailed to the land with the bong trees,
There were lots of insects like wasps and bees.
When they arrived they couldn't decide
Whether to stay or leave.
Then they had an agreement, they decided to stay
Then one day they got lost and became astray.
So there you have it, two men stranded on a beach
With nothing to eat except one peach.
They fought and fought for days and days
over the silky peach
They never knew how hard life was living on a beach.

Gemma Freeman (10)
St Bartholomew's RC Primary School, Prescot

HORSES AND PONIES

H is for hooves that gallop and trot.
O is for oats that horses like a lot.
R is for reins you have to hold.
S is for saddle sometimes new sometimes old.
E is for each stirrup that swings side to side.
S is for Sandy a horse that I ride.

A is for apples to have as a treat.
N is for neigh when they want to eat.
D is for Don a breed of a horse.

P is for Palomino a pony of course.
O is for over the jumps we go.
N is for nostrils that snort and blow.
I is for Ireland where Connemaras come from.
E is for an Exmoor who is called Tom.
S is for socks which some have on their feet.

A is for Arab which are very neat.
R is for rosettes that are won in shows.
E is for ears and N is for nose.

C is for canter, a horse's pace.
O is for oh what a cute little face.
O is for old horses that go lame.
L is for love that matters all the same.

Jessica Skidmore (10)
St Bartholomew's RC Primary School, Prescot

WHEN WINTER COMES

It's very cold and breezy,
It's very damp and dreary,
I can't go out to play,
Because the rain's coming this way.

I'm wearing my gloves,
And I'm wearing my hat,
And when I come in,
There's a warm welcome mat.

Paul Banks (10)
St Bartholomew's RC Primary School, Prescot

THE WINTER SEASON

The winter is here
There is no cheer
The leaves are falling all around
It's like a carpet on the ground.

The trees are now bare
They haven't a care
For they will now sleep
Until spring is here.

When it gets cold
You worry about the old
Especially our grandparents
With just one slip
They could break a hip.

The snow will soon
Begin to fall
Then we will have fun
Making snowballs.

It is now winter
The bees are dead
We're all snug in our beds.

Georgina Smithwick (10)
St Bartholomew's RC Primary School, Prescot

CREEPY SPOOKS AND EERIE GHOSTS

It's hard to say which I fear the most
A creepy spook or an eerie ghost,
They're often seen in the middle of the night
Nearly always dressed in white.

They flit and float without a sound,
I can always tell when they're around,
Because I wake up from my sleep,
And feel my flesh begin to creep,
My heart begins to fill with fear,
I know the dreaded ghost is here.

Up I jump and give a cry,
'Help help! a ghost is nigh'
I run down the stairs with one huge leap,
And find myself out in the street,
'Was it just a dream?' I say,
'Or can't I keep the ghosts at bay?'

Richard Teebay (11)
St Bartholomew's RC Primary School, Prescot

HENRY VII

Henry VII was very thin
But he never put his money in the bin
He married Elizabeth of York
She always ate a lot of pork
Arthur died, Henry's son
But Henry was not very much fun.

Rebecca Sandeman (8)
St Bartholomew's RC Primary School, Prescot

HENRY VII POEM

Henry VII was a very good man.
He always ate salad sandwiches with ham.
He stopped all wars
With his great big oars.
He had long black hair and big blue eyes
And everyone thought he was wise.
Henry VII was very thin
He had a very big chin.
His flag was red and white
He always carried a bright light.
He didn't dress in kings' clothes
He also had a great big nose.
He didn't have a crown of jewels
He wouldn't let people break the rules.
The Battle of Bosworth was the end
For Henry Tudor, king and friend.

Nicole Flexen (8)
St Bartholomew's RC Primary School, Prescot

BOYS

Pushing, shoving and a big loud yell
Why do boys always smell?
Racing, running round and round
They even push you to the ground
Having pet spiders and picking their noses
And kicking the neighbours' roses
I think the world would be a better place
If we flush the boys down the toilet without a trace!

Olivia Kane-Frazer (7)
St Bartholomew's RC Primary School, Prescot

MINNIE THE OGRE

Minnie the ogre lives in a cave,
With a load of carrots,
She made carrot pudding and carrot brew,
You should have seen them, they were yucky.

Minnie the ogre has a car.
It is very small,
But she went quite fast,
You should have seen the police,
They were chasing like mad.

Minnie the ogre is still asleep,
Tucked up in her special bed,
Everybody be quiet, *shhhh,*
Let's say goodnight.

Darren Devonport (10)
St Bartholomew's RC Primary School, Prescot

MY DREAM

Pigs are flying in my dream,
While I'm eating big ice-creams.
Wind is swirling all around,
Even so there is no sound.
Then I'm swimming in a pool,
Then I'm watching Liverpool,
Sitting, sneezing, coughing, wheezing,
These things are happening while I'm dreaming.

Kevin Byron (11)
St Bartholomew's RC Primary School, Prescot

THE MONSTER

I see a monster
It is twenty feet long
Every time I sniff, its feet pong
Scared to move an inch away
It creeps closer to me every day
It's green with a black and white spot
In the dark it seems to hop
It takes a leap
I scream out loud
No one hears me
So the dog howled
My mum runs in
There's nothing there
It must be behind the crooked chair.

Ian Morris (9)
St Bartholomew's RC Primary School, Prescot

MY SISTER!

My baby sister is two years old
She is good as gold
She is smelly but not very old
She is rough
And she tumbles down the stairs
First she is bald, next she's got gallons of hair
So I love my sister through thick and thin
So Siobahn I love you.

Michael Gittins (10)
St Bartholomew's RC Primary School, Prescot

A WINTER POEM

Cold nights and frosty mornings
Foggy days come without warning
We can't play out
It's totally boring

We wake up one morning
Snowflakes have fallen overnight
Crisp white snow
Oh what a sight!

We get out our sledges
And go to the park
Oh it's great!
We play till it's dark.

Alex McCracken (10)
St Bartholomew's RC Primary School, Prescot

MY FAVOURITE HOBBY IS POOL

I have a hobby which is playing pool
But this is not allowed when I am at school
That is a rule
No time to shoot pool.

Even when I come home from school
There is a rule
'Homework first or you will end up a fool'
And at weekends I get to play pool.

Paul Bennett (10)
St Bartholomew's RC Primary School, Prescot

WINTERTIME

Winter, winter, snow on the ground,
Ice is forming all around,
All the lakes begin to freeze,
Soon we'll all begin to sneeze.

Winter, winter, children play,
Some in the snow, some on the sleigh,
Building snowmen makes them smile,
They hope the snow will last a while.

Winter, winter, long dark nights,
Cold dark mornings, Jack Frost bites,
Children's footprints in the snow,
Warm fires at home with flames that glow.

Emma Vose (9)
St Bartholomew's RC Primary School, Prescot

HENRY VII

Henry VII was slim and tall
He lived in a mansion with a great big hall
Henry a'hunting he did not like
He would rather stay at home flying a kite
He wore rings of gold until he grew very old
Henry was classed second-rate
Because he was a miser and a cheapskate
He wore a crown which always fell down
Because his hair was thin and brown.

David Carroll (8)
St Bartholomew's RC Primary School, Prescot

WINTER

The skies are grey,
The leaves are falling.
It's getting cold,
Winter's calling.

No more sandals,
No more skirts
Get out woolly jumpers,
Get out thermal shirts.

No more ice-creams,
No more Coke
Time for hot chocolate,
It's not a joke!

Jenny Ardrey (10)
St Bartholomew's RC Primary School, Prescot

HENRY VII

Henry VII was a very good king.
He did his best for everyone and everything.
He gained his crown at the battle of Bosworth.
After defeating Richard III.
He reigned from 1485 to 1509.
He celebrated with a glass of wine.
He united the houses of York and Lancaster,
By his marriage to Elizabeth of York
After he asked her.

Michael Arrowsmith (7)
St Bartholomew's RC Primary School, Prescot

WINTER POEM

Autumn has gone,
Spring has gone,
Guess how many leaves are left?
None!

All the air's cold,
It would be in this time of the year,
All the men go out,
To get some beer.

Everybody's in shops,
So am I,
All the birds have gone,
They've gone to fly.

Heather Winstanley (9)
St Bartholomew's RC Primary School, Prescot

HORSES AND PONIES

Horses, ponies all around,
They cheer me up when I am down.
I ride them all the year through,
And even if I've got the flu.

They are sleek and they are fast,
They have lived for years of past.
Their fur is soft and silky too,
I love them really,
Yes I do.

Susan Cairns (10)
St Bartholomew's RC Primary School, Prescot

GIRLS

There are girls at home
There are girls at school
There are girls that think
They're really cool.

In the school hols all they do
Is play with dolls.

Mopping and shopping is
What girls do best
While I just have a rest.

I'll say it once, I'll say it twice
Girls are not really nice.

Lewis Harris (8)
St Bartholomew's RC Primary School, Prescot

THE ANT

Ants are small,
Ants are tall,
Ants can drive me up the wall!

They work all day,
No rest, no play,
Scurrying, hurrying all the day!

You find them in the strangest places,
Under a stone, on their own,
I think they're funny but annoying so I tell them to just *go away!*

Helen Rothwell (10)
St Bartholomew's RC Primary School, Prescot

MY POEM

My best friend is Katie
She is my favourite matie
She goes to gymnastics
She is fantastic
She has a little sister
Katie says she's a blister

My second friend is Emma
We all call her Emmy
She had a friend called Jenny
Her mum is called Cassie
She had a dog called Lassie
They are my best friends.

Jodie Coughlan (10)
St Bartholomew's RC Primary School, Prescot

MY TUDOR POEM

Henry VIII had hair of brown.
On Bosworth his dad was given a crown.
Henry VIII had diamonds on his clothes.
But of course they were sewn on in rows.
He sailed out with his oars.
Sometimes he made new laws.
Henry VIII had six wives.
He always told lies.
He thought he was very wise.
He treated people like a toy.
All he wanted was a boy.

Tom Coghlan (7)
St Bartholomew's RC Primary School, Prescot

TREES ARE WONDERFUL!

Trees, trees are wonderful things,
They're part of our environment.
They have branches, bark and a trunk,
But most of all trees have leaves.

Trees, trees are wonderful things,
They make great homes for animals.
Squirrels, birds, even woodlice like trees
So why can't humans like them too?
Trees, trees are wonderful things,
But humans cut them down.
We can still save the trees,
If we campaign around!

Phillip Brougham (11)
St Bartholomew's RC Primary School, Prescot

HENRY VII

Henry VII was a very wise king
He did trades in everything

He was happy and handsome and rich
and good

He helped the poor as much as he could

Elizabeth of York was Henry's wife
They had a very exciting life

Arthur was Henry's son
He married Catherine of Aragon.

Anthony Freeman (7)
St Bartholomew's RC Primary School, Prescot

MY HOBBY

My hobby is, can you guess what?
It's riding
Yes I like that a lot.

The horse I am on is called Spot
He is lazy
And I have to use my crop.

He eats everything he can find
He puts down his neck
And I end up on his hind.

I have often dreamed of being on the top
In the race's riding spot.

Today I'm teaching Spot
How to do a perfect trot.

Tomorrow is a test
And I'm going to do my best.

Guess what, I passed
But my poor friend came last.

And now I can enter the race
But I have to ride a horse called Grace.

In the race I came second
Just as I reckoned.

I'll be entering again
So watch out for me on your TV.

Holly McCarthy (9)
St Bartholomew's RC Primary School, Prescot

HENRY VII

Henry VII had hair of brown
On a Bosworth field he was given a crown
He kept his money, he ate his honey
He paid his jesters for being funny
He fought with Richard who died that day
'No more wars;' Henry did pray
The house of Lancaster now ruled the land
He married Elizabeth who took his hand
The people liked this peaceful king
His new laws and everything
Henry VII was kind and great
But watch out for Henry number 8.

Thomas Meredith (7)
St Bartholomew's RC Primary School, Prescot

LOVE LOST

The church stood empty, creaky doors opened wide,
Husband to be cried and cried,
Old sandy walls listened to guests that had sighed,
Because the bride to be had suddenly died.

Worn slate tiles barely stop wind and rain,
Attempts to mend have failed once again,
Gravestones sit like decaying teeth,
Groom wonders why all this unwanted grief.

Wheelbarrow squeaks like it needed an oil,
As the gardener strolled by to dig stony soil,
Not to plant flowers or rake golden hay,
But to bury a bride on her wedding day.

Claire Latham (10)
St Joseph's RC Primary School, Wallasey

SEVEN-YEAR ITCH

An old man sat in a graveyard,
Scratching his itchy itch,
Wondering what it would be like,
If he was famous and rich.

But all he had was a penny,
To buy his food and drink,
His hair was thin and wispy,
From his boots a terrible stink.

The old man felt so lonely,
He didn't have a friend,
And he was also ugly,
Which drove him round the bend.

A young girl sat beside him,
And slipped her hand in his,
Don't feel so sad and gloomy,
It's bad to be like this.

They talked there for a while,
About his worries and woes,
And he began to think,
Fight back at what life throws.

She left him then to ponder,
The things they had discussed,
And scratching his itchy itch he said,
Change my ways I really must.

Ellen McGinley (10)
St Joseph's RC Primary School, Wallasey

THE BIG ISSUE

I may be dressed in rags but really I'm not all that bad,
I'm usually quite pleasant but I know lately I've been sad,
Sorry if you don't like me but a troubled time I've had.

Buy the Big Issue,
Buy the Big Issue,
Oi! Get away from that grave,
Buy the Big Issue,
Buy the Big Issue,
I need pennies to save.

Why did it have to be me, the unlucky one?
My money, my house and my wife all gone,
Now it's just dinner and tea for one.

Buy the Big Issue,
Buy the Big Issue,
Oi! Get away from that grave,
Buy the Big Issue,
Buy the Big Issue,
I need pennies to save.

Why in the graveyard I hear you ask?
Well I like to be near her, now she's under the grass,
We always talked before she suddenly passed.

Buy the Big Issue,
Buy the Big Issue,
Oi! Get away from that grave,
Buy the Big Issue,
Buy the Big Issue,
I need pennies to save.

Please, please help, all I want's a few pence,
It'll be a start and a bit of a chance,
So give me a reason to get up and dance.

Buy the Big Issue,
Buy the Big Issue,
Oi! Get away from that grave,
Buy the Big Issue,
Buy the Big Issue,
I need pennies to save.

Gemma Morton (10)
St Joseph's RC Primary School, Wallasey

THE HIDDEN MESSAGE

Leaning like an old man with a poor back,
many passers-by on the long dusty track.
Wheat blowing with its golden straggly hair,
People trampling over it without a care.
Bushes green with prickly sides,
Secret messages within they hide.
Proud tree standing tall,
Beckoning nature with its call.
Tree wrapped in moistened bark,
Above the wheat swoops a magnificent lark.
Earth's beautiful countryside,
Is where Mother Nature's secrets hide.
Fragile is nature's face,
So look after it with caring embrace.
Don't forget that nature speaks,
Hurt it much and it grows weak.
The important message I send to you,
Treat nature fine and well and true.

James McGowan (11)
St Joseph's RC Primary School, Wallasey

PET DOG SAVES THE DAY

The beaten prince strips off his armour
and lifts a sword to kill,
The kingdom's enemies are winning
and he has lost the will.

Kind wife is feeling worried
Old king's looking strange,
Mad dog is startled by the fuss
and quickly goes insane.

The traitor trembles in the corner
ready for the rumble,
But George is feeling rather faint
and he's about to crumble.

Then suddenly the rabid hound
leaps in to make a rescue,
he sinks his fangs in traitor's flesh
Big bones for tea as thank you!

Michael Davies (10)
St Joseph's RC Primary School, Wallasey

THE STARTLED RABBIT

The startled rabbit squeezes through cracks in gigantic boulders,
Crunching chestnut-coloured leaves as he scampers by,
And feeling terribly afraid that he's going to die.
Thin puny trees bent and crooked like old people's legs,
Wave through the wind at passers-by,
While hungry birds flock south to meet the sun again.
Tufts of yellow grass stand like men on crutches,
And amongst the prickly bushes the rabbit is hidden,
Waiting to burrow where man is forbidden.

Bradley McGovern (11)
St Joseph's RC Primary School, Wallasey

PLAYING HARD TO GET

Her tumbling tresses shine so bright
Prince Charming pleads with this magical sight
The golden ring flies through the air
Which Princess Tina tossed, she doesn't care

Lily pads float weightless on the pond
As Prince Charming tries to mend the bond
These two have rowed a terrible row
To make it up he wants but how?

Hands clasped tightly and on his knees
He begs the princess, forgive me please
But she just pouts and pulls a face
She likes to tease and play the chase.

Barry Murphy (11)
St Joseph's RC Primary School, Wallasey

PREPARING FOR A BANQUET

In the king's palace a swan lies still like a white fluffy pillow,
and a red juicy apple rolls like a tennis ball.
The cat's eyes sparkle like emerald-green marbles,
and ten tin pans shine like mirrors leaning on the wall.
As a dad bird waits to be plucked bare to its skin,
servants are busy preparing the lavish banquet dinner.
The maids clothed in black and white uniform dressed,
lift cold heavy china down from great wooden cupboards.
Guests are getting hungry as they wait for their food,
it's chaos in the kitchen and the butler's in a mood.

Richard Palin (11)
St Joseph's RC Primary School, Wallasey

HEROES LEFT BEHIND

As the ship comes in,
Brave soldiers stand, with grief and pride,
Their thoughts and feelings quite hard to hide,
The anchor drops now, to depths below,
And the horn blows.

As the ship comes in,
Loyal wives stand, looking up above,
Their fears and worries smothered in love,
The gangway drops now, to let men go,
For land and sea are joined.

As the ship comes in,
Sad children stand, crying tears of hate,
Their fathers met a bloody fate,
The sails drop now, the wind has died,
Just like those heroes left behind.

Billy Hopkins (10)
St Joseph's RC Primary School, Wallasey

FLOWER POWER

Farmer Powers loved his flowers,
He planted them with thought,
Fertile soil and sunlight's rays,
Were what he carefully sought.

Farmer Powers loved his flowers,
He watered them with pride,
Straight and strong the stems will grow,
Red petals will not hide.

Farmer Powers loved his flowers,
He pruned them with respect,
Cut and shaped the best he could,
Those thorns they will protect.

Farmer Powers loved his flowers,
He gazed at them with pleasure,
Wishing that they could stay,
Like this now and forever.

Natalie Lucas (11)
St Joseph's RC Primary School, Wallasey

AN OLD ROOM IN THE PALACE

At the king's palace
in an old dusty room,
the birds flew in
through a hole in the roof,
as the cats sat and watched
with a sparkle in their eyes.
A mother and son stood still in despair,
as they looked at the cats,
stalking birds in the air.
So they threw some fruit,
that scared them away,
sat down to eat and
enjoy the rest of the day.
When evening came,
and everybody slept,
the mice woke up,
and nibbled all that was left.

Sean Charlesworth (11)
St Joseph's RC Primary School, Wallasey

KEEPING WATCH

With rosy cheeks like apples
And hair like balls of dust
The child sleeps on Mother's lap
Rest she really must

The fire is burning brightly
It warms them through the night
While Mother keeps watch for danger
Until dawn of morning light

Child looks so very peaceful
It's surely a happy dream
But Mother's face is troubled
Worried eyes with telling gleam.

Sarah Griffiths (10)
St Joseph's RC Primary School, Wallasey

A SAD DAY

The sun is out and summer's here
Butterfly's wounded, shed a tear
Not for you a happy day
Your time has gone you cannot stay

Bushes and birds and pretty flowers
Make us happy for hours and hours
The sea is calm and very bright
No bobbing boats today in sight

Tree trunk standing tall and strong
Dropping leaves all along
Cold and windy, dull and stark
It will soon be very dark

The sand, it moves and runs away
Sea waves gently in the bay
It gets dark and we must run
Home to Mum and tea we come.

Alexander Breen (11)
St Joseph's RC Primary School, Wallasey

MELANCHOLY

The mother and the child sit
With bright cheeks like rosy apples
And gloomy eyes stare in despair

The mother and the child sit
Beside rows of old houses
That look like deserted churches

The mother and the child sit
They sit sadly waiting for help
Whilst the glistening fire burns bright

They are lonely, they are homeless
They have nowhere to go.

Jenna Price (10)
St Joseph's RC Primary School, Wallasey

ESCAPE

Castle crumbles to its final remains,
As panicking people scream for loved ones,
Desperately fleeing the red burning furnace,
Which tried to clutch them in its hot red flames.

Boats bulge with hysterical folk,
Clinging close to one another for comfort,
As haggard horses wade through icy waters,
Scurrying soldiers splutter their way out of smoke.

Weapons wobble in trembling hands,
Eagle eyes search frantically for danger,
Injured bleed through bandaged wounds,
And children cry for lost homelands.

Andrew Parry (10)
St Joseph's RC Primary School, Wallasey

AFTERNOON TEA

The dog is feeling playful,
Wondering what is up,
He hates anything quiet,
'Cos Patch is just a pup.

The lady at the window,
Smiles sweetly at her guests,
Tea is on the table,
It's in the china best.

The garden in the distance,
Reveals its golden glory,
As ivy taps the window pane,
The husband starts his story.

The room is warm and cosy,
And Mother wants to snore,
Wondering why on earth her daughter,
Married such a bore.

Beckie Cleary (10)
St Joseph's RC Primary School, Wallasey

THE SINGING SWALLOW

Singing brightly the swallow swoops suddenly from above,
And with fluttering wings it brings freedom for love,
Hovering like a rescue helicopter over the dark prison cell,
He sings merrily the message he came to tell.

As clanking chains rattle and rub against blistered feet,
The weary prisoner hungers vainly for morsels to eat,
A face so pale and showing the pain,
Of being locked away from his loved one again.

Iron bars in the window separate these two,
What, thinks the swallow, can he possibly do,
How can he tell them that he's able to see,
The jailer is coming to set someone free.

Christopher King (10)
St Joseph's RC Primary School, Wallasey

IDEAS FROM MY PAINTBOX

Blue is the colour of
The sky like the ocean wide.
Blue is the colour of
A lovely calm swimming pool.
Blue is the colour of
A wrestling ring rumbling as loud as the crowd.
Blue is the colour of
The Everton home kit like the sparkling sky.

Red is the colour of
Blood oozing out of a cut hand.
Red is the colour of the
Liverpool home kit red as cherries.
Red is the colour of
A fire flickering in the night.
Red is the colour of
A rosy apple shining in the tree.

Green is the colour of
Grass blowing in the wind.
Green is the colour of
A snake sliding in the forest.
Green is the colour of
A frog jumping on the leaves in the pond.
Green is the colour of
Someone's green eyes staring at you.

Yellow is the colour of
A beautiful daffodil growing in the garden.
Yellow is the colour of
A desert, the sand blowing in the wind.

Yellow is the colour of
A beautiful juicy banana.
Yellow is the colour of
The sun shining over the sea.

Christian Thomas (10)
St Laurence's RC Primary School, Kirkby

IDEAS FROM MY PAINTBOX

Blue is the colour of a bluebell flower which blows gently
in the wind.
Blue is the colour of a bluebird gliding through the nice breeze.
Blue is the colour of a sticky sweet which tingles your tongue and
tastes
Gorgeous!
Blue is the colour of ink as it splots on the paper making funny shapes

Red is the colour of a rose
Blossoming from its stem in the bright sun
Red is the colour of an apple high up in a big tree
As red as a rose and as juicy as an orange
Red is the colour of a sweet cherry hanging from a tree
in the summer's hot sun
Red is the colour of the Liverpool home kit,
As red as the devil but not as naughty

Brown is the colour of a lion roaring loudly in the dark night sky
Brown is the colour of bark on an old tree as old as time can be
Brown is the colour of chocolate melting in my warm hands
next to a hot fire
Brown is the colour of a tawny owl whooshing through the air
like a kite.

Jonnie Brennan (10)
St Laurence's RC Primary School, Kirkby

IDEAS FROM MY PAINTBOX

Blue is the colour of
The sea raging in a fierce storm.
The sky sparkling on a spring morn.
Eyes as blue as blue could be.
Blue eyes is what I have like the clear clear sea.

Red is the colour of
The macaw flying in the wind
Liverpool's scarlet red kit dashing from goal to goal.
Firelight flames flickering like they're dancing.
A rosy red apple falling from a huge old apple tree.

Yellow is the colour of Liverpool's yellow away kit
Beating Barnsley even though they scored in the
opening seven minutes.
My custard yellow creative writing book I am writing
this poem in.
The new daffodils emerging from the sun-warmed soil
Stars shining on a clear summer's night.

Orange is the colour of
Lewis' hair as he scores a brilliant goal.
Or David James' Liverpool goal kit that he's saved
some brilliant goals in.
A sweet juicy orange that seems to melt in your mouth.
The sun so orange like a ball of flame that never
seems to die.

John Campbell (10)
St Laurence's RC Primary School, Kirkby

FROST

Freezing, fragile, falls from the sky
Ring of ice
Off the clouds
Slow from the sky
Taking over the world with its cold breath.

Nicola Jones (9)
St Laurence's RC Primary School, Kirkby

FUNNY POEM

If I was a bird
My wings I would spread
I'd swoop over you
And plop on your head.

Neil James Phillips (9)
St Laurence's RC Primary School, Kirkby

WINDY AND SNOWY

When it is windy, it's cold and icy.
When it snows, it's freezing and deep.
When it hails, it hits our windows.
When it thunders, it makes a horrible rumbling noise.

Jo Louise Cain (10)
St Laurence's RC Primary School, Kirkby

IDEAS FROM MY PAINTBOX

Blue is the colour of a waving balloon floating
up into the sky.
Blue is the colour of all the blue on the globe.
Blue is the colour of the kit Everton wear.
Blue is the colour of a wrestling ring, a lovely sky blue.

Red is the colour of
The Liverpool kit glowing each time I wear it.
Red is the colour of
An apple, a juicy round fruit.
Red is the colour of pigs, a smelly old couple!
Red is the colour of a fire
A red flaming thing.

Orange is the colour of the sparkling sun
shining and shining.
Orange is the colour of my friend's hair
A dark, dark orange.
Orange is the colour of the rug in my class.
Orange is the colour of my Cambridge maths book
A light, light orange.

Craig Noone (10)
St Laurence's RC Primary School, Kirkby

WINTER

W inter comes just once a year,
I   n the winter snow appears,
N ext day it's still there,
T omorrow all is clear,
E ver since been windy and wet,
R ather have more snow though.

Gemma McGorian (11)
St Laurence's RC Primary School, Kirkby

MY SPECIAL MUM

My mum is special in every way,
She loves and cares for me every single day,
She makes me feel happy and glad
When I am feeling very sad.
Her laughs and smiles are so cheerful,
With her shouts so so hearful.
When I have a headache or even when I'm ill,
She'll run to the cupboards and find some medicine for me.
Dreams and hopes she hears,
Until they become so clear.
Treats she buys me but only when I'm good,
So I try really hard until I really could.
My mum is really good to me
She forgives me straight away,
So now I've got to get her a gift
Because Mother's Day is on its way.
Mother's Day is here now,
And going very fast,
So all I've got to say is that
It's been a blast.

Rachel Reid (10)
St Laurence's RC Primary School, Kirkby

OUR HEADMASTER

Tiptoe down the stairs
Tap, tap, along the corridor
Squeak, squeak, to the foyer
Turn into the headmaster's office
All I can see are the footballers scoring
All I can hear is the headmaster roaring

Stevi Jones (9)
St Laurence's RC Primary School, Kirkby

THE BIG MATCH

Duncan Ferguson has
the ball he
is sure not
to fall.
He passed to
Speed
Speed to
the floor
and camaraderie went out the door.

Ferguson got
the ball and then
he went to the goal
and it was
a successful score.
The crowd cheered
and everyone was in tears
because Duncan Ferguson
has scored his hat trick.

Craig Davidson (8)
St Laurence's RC Primary School, Kirkby

FROST

It is white and misty.
It looks like snow and it is very cold.
It reminds me of winter and Christmas.
It isn't used for anything.
It is very light and delicate.
It is frost.

Emma-Jayne Moore (9)
St Laurence's RC Primary School, Kirkby

RAIN, SNOW, WIND

Rain in my fingers,
Rain in my toes,
Rain in my ears,
Rain up my nose.
Oh, I do hate the rain.

Snow in my hat,
Snow in my scarf,
Snow in my gloves,
Snow in my wellies.
Oh, I do like it when it snows
so I can build a snowman.

Wind in my hair,
Wind in the trees.
Wind is a gale,
Or is wind just a breeze?
Oh winter, please go away
so I can go outside to play.

Hayley Durkin (11)
St Laurence's RC Primary School, Kirkby

MY SPECIAL MUM

My mum is special as special as can be
Whenever I'm in trouble she's always there for me,
Or even when I'm feeling down and looking rather sad
And when I lose my temper and I get really mad.
If I need a shoulder to cry on
She's the best mum to rely on.
So I would just like to say
Have a special Mother's Day!

Amy Maguire (10)
St Laurence's RC Primary School, Kirkby

MOTHER

M y mum is magnificent in every way.

O nly the one at home I love.

T houghtful and true to me.

H onest and truthful in every way.

E ver-loving just for me.

R esponsible just for me.

Natalie Atkins (10)
St Laurence's RC Primary School, Kirkby

FROST!

It is like a white stone.

It looks like an ice rink.

It reminds me of snow because

it is the same colour.

It isn't used for anything.

It is *frost*.

Katie Brooks (9)
St Laurence's RC Primary School, Kirkby

MOTHER

M y mum is so magnificent,

O nly my mum can make me happy,

T errific and talented,

H er heart is honest,

E very time my mum is there,

R especting and loving me when I am near her.

Robert Hughes (10)
St Laurence's RC Primary School, Kirkby

WINTER DAYS

Winter days are very cold
They make you run all the way home
The white snow falls softly to the ground
I hope it stays here all year round
When you stand up you fall back down
The snow is freezing so are you
The snow falls heavily and blows hard into my face.

Lesleyann Whiteside (11)
St Laurence's RC Primary School, Kirkby

MY MUM

My mum is so special.
She cares, hugs and buys for me.
My mum is so kind
She comforts, helps and shares with me.
My mum sometimes shouts at me
Because I drive her up the wall.
But my mum is the best mum
In the whole wide world.
Whenever I am hurt,
As hurt, as hurt can be
My mum is always there for me.
But the best thing about my mum is that
She loves me dearly.

Stephanie Jennings (11)
St Laurence's RC Primary School, Kirkby

IDEAS FROM MY PAINTBOX

Blue is the colour of bluebirds sweetly singing in the sky.
Blue is the colour of the reflecting waves going very high.
Blue is the colour of the bright blue sky.
Blue is the colour of my bright blue eyes.

Red is the colour of the blood pouring out of a cut.
Red is the colour of a big mean fox hiding in its hut.
Red is the colour of a sweet juicy apple crunched by teeth.
Red is the colour of an autumn leaf.

Green is the colour of long streaks of grass.
Green is the colour of the trees shining like glass.
Green is the colour of a sour big apple bitten by teeth.
Green is the colour of a summer leaf.

Yellow is the colour of the bright big sun.
Yellow is the colour of me as bright as my mum.
Yellow is the colour of some of the birds.
Yellow is the colour of tweeting beaks.

Rebecca Tracey (10)
St Laurence's RC Primary School, Kirkby

WINTER

Rain is bad, that makes you sad.
Winter is cold, not for the old.
Freezing cold snow, footprints though, I don't know.
Stormy nights, that give you a fright.
Snow is white, what a lovely sight.
Noisy hail, that makes you pale.
Curtains drawn, nice and warm.
Wrapped and cosy, nice and rosy.
Lots of heat, with something to eat.

Charlotte McIver (10)
St Laurence's RC Primary School, Kirkby

IDEAS FROM MY PAINTBOX

Blue is the colour of the gentle waves
flowing from side to side.
Blue is the colour of my friend's eyes
flickering in the light.
Blue is the colour of the big blue
dolphins splashing in the sea.
Blue is the colour of the sky lovely and bright,
with clouds all in-between.

Red is the colour of the blood of your hand
when you have cut it open.
Red is the colour of the Liverpool football kit,
Red as roses.
Red is the colour of my friend's lips
Red as berries.
Red is the colour of
the sun when it is setting in the sky.

Valerie McCaffery (10)
St Laurence's RC Primary School, Kirkby

MY MUM IS SO SPECIAL

My mum is special, she makes the world go round,
Whenever I'm ill, she never makes a sound.

My mum is so special, so kind, so loving, she cares,
She always hopes the best for me, because I know she really cares.

Whenever I go out, she always looks around for me,
Whenever I'm in school, she flies around like a bumble bee.

Sometimes she will shout at me, or sometimes give me treats,
And when I mean treats, she will give me a lot of sweets.

Dean Kenny (11)
St Laurence's RC Primary School, Kirkby

IDEAS FROM MY PAINTBOX

Blue is the colour of sapphires,
Like the sky brighter than bright.
Blue is the colour of a blueberry
So yummy for my tummy.
Blue is the colour of a blue shark waiting for its prey
Blue is the colour of a kingfisher perched ready
to spring into action.

Red is the colour of the Liverpool home kit
Like a rosy apple,
It could be blood oozing out of a cut,
It could be flames dancing.

Black is the colour of your darkest fears,
It could be darkness closing in,
It could be ink spilling down a page
It could be oil killing sea life.

Paul McCormick (10)
St Laurence's RC Primary School, Kirkby

MY COUSIN JENIFFER

My cousin is kind
My cousin is funny
She cheers me up
When I am glum
She buys me presents
She buys me clothes
She takes me here
She takes me there
She takes me everywhere
I love my cousin, she loves me.

Jodi Frackleton (8)
St Laurence's RC Primary School, Kirkby

MY MUM

My mum is so special,
She's always there for me,
Whenever I'm in trouble,
She always listens to me.

My mum is so special,
She shares her time with me,
Whenever I am ill,
She always looks after me.

My mum sometimes shouts at me,
Because I drive her up the wall,
But in the end she forgives me,
I'm her daughter after all.

Mum, I'd just like to say,
Happy Mother's Day!

Kelly Harrington (11)
St Laurence's RC Primary School, Kirkby

MUMS

Mums are the best.
Caring and sharing.
Loving us all so dearly.
Shout at us for a reason.
She has always been my friend.
She keeps me healthy every day.
She is always there for me.
She always forgives me
whenever I am in trouble.
She always sticks up for me.

Tracey Occamore (10)
St Laurence's RC Primary School, Kirkby

DONNA'S POEM

D oing the cleaning all day long.
　　My mum is a worker
　　And she likes a good singsong.

O r if she's in a good mood,
　　She'll give me toys and lots of food.

N aughty or nice she thinks I'm shy,
　　She'll treat me nice if I don't tell a lie.

N ever feeling dull, always happy and cheerful,
　　She listens to whatever I say
　　Even if I talk all day.

A loving mother who shouts sometimes.
　　She's not like teachers,
　　She doesn't give you lines.

Christopher Carney (11)
St Laurence's RC Primary School, Kirkby

MY MUM

My mum is very special
I love her with all my heart
My mum is so special, special as can be
She takes me to visit people and feeds me my tea
I love my mum and she loves me.

My mum is very special
But she shouts at me
When she comes to see me, she says 'I'm sorry, do you forgive me?'
I love my mum and she loves me.

My mum is very special so special as can be
Whenever I'm in trouble, she's always there for me
My mum is very special to me
I love my mum and she loves me.

Rebecca Fairclough (11)
St Laurence's RC Primary School, Kirkby

THE TOILET

Down in the toilet where everyone goes,
lives an ant who everyone knows.
He goes to the toilet, washes his hands,
has a drink, dries his hands.
Throws loads of paper towels in the bin,
that's the ant everyone knows.
Down in the toilet where everyone goes,
lives a buzzy bumble bee,
who eats loads and loads.
He loves omelettes made with cheese,
that's the bee everyone knows.
Down in the toilet where everyone goes,
there's an elephant who trumpets,
and squash squash, the ant and bee are *gone!*
Down in the toilet where now, nobody goes.

Scott McGiveron (9)
St Laurence's RC Primary School, Kirkby

THE ONE AND ONLY

T he one and only is my mum
H elping me when I'm sick
E ven when she's busy at work.

O ver and over again
N ever saying thank you
E very day she gives me things.

A nd never ever complains
N o one gives anything except a little hug
D oing things we shouldn't.

O ver and over again
N ever saying sorry
L oving you Mum with all my heart
Y ou are the one and only for me.

Ellen Stuart (11)
St Laurence's RC Primary School, Kirkby

MOTHER

M y mum is a miracle machine.
O nly she has the talent of a mother.
T errific tea drinker is she.
H appy hearty mother.
E lect my mother for world's greatest mum.
R eward my mother with a remarkable trophy.

Martin O'Neil (10)
St Laurence's RC Primary School, Kirkby

MY CLASS

My teacher is Miss Chalkley
very pretty, never naughty.
Maria, very hard worker,
Thomas, always clumsy,
Scot, very noisy,
Mark, too,
Martin, the smart one,
Neil, the tough one,
Emma, always smiling,
Kelly, the worrier,
Carla, the giggler, just like me,
Rhianon, always talking,
Bella, laughing with Emma,
and me. The giggling never ends.

James (9)
St Laurence's RC Primary School, Kirkby

MOTHER

M y mum is marvellous
O nly special mum around
T ender and terrific always
H andy and helpful all day long
E very day there for me
R ather think about us than herself.
   You won the best mum competition.

Courtney Croker (10)
St Laurence's RC Primary School, Kirkby

My Teacher The Secret Agent!

My teacher, Miss Chalkley is a
Secret Agent.
She searches us for money and gold.
She's a really sneaky thief!
She goes into the staff room
And eats biscuits.
I think they talk about us.
Oh no! Where have all my mates gone?
Miss has stolen them.
She'll put them up for ransom.
Well I'm glad I'm still here.
Ahhhhhhh!
Help she's taken me too!

Jessica Carney (9)
St Laurence's RC Primary School, Kirkby

Red Sun In The Sky

Red sun in the sky,
Blackbirds and starlings fly so high.
In the lovely sweet fresh air,
The smell of corn is everywhere.

Then suddenly I hear a cry,
A howling then a squeal and sigh.

All is calm and quiet again,
But I feel a very sharp pain.

Now it's nigh,
And there's no sign
Of anybody,
Around or by.

Helen Brankin (11)
St Luke's CE Primary School, Formby

IN THE HAYFIELD

Standing on top of the hay cart, knee-deep in the wonderful hay
I look around the hayfield, oh what a beautiful day.

Suddenly the peace is shattered, I hear from not too far,
Frederick teasing Johnny, tickeldy, pouffella ha.

Mister Johnny picks up a pitchfork and points it straight at Fred,
I close my eyes and hear Albert cry out,
                    but I'm deep in the darkness blotted with red.

When I finally open my eyes I see Johnny crying so sad,
And horrible, mean and evil Fred saying that Johnny is mad.

Suddenly 'cross the wispy straw comes Mrs Gotobed
Dressed in a silvery ball gown with feathers on that are red.

'Well Miss Emerald Eyes are you having fun,
Helping in my hay field and playing in the sun?'

'Yes, Mrs Gotobed, everything's fine,
But I really do think that your dress is divine.'

'Thank you child, this is the last,
It reminds me of some good times past.'

She turns away, walks through the hay, leaning on Hepzibah's arm.
Frederick starts working again, my world returns to calm.

Heather Constantine (11)
St Luke's CE Primary School, Formby

THE SEA DRAGON

The sea dragon starts to stir
From his bed of seaweed.
He spits out clear white foam
From his mouth of blue-green.

He lets out a mighty bellow
He rises and makes a tidal wave.
Many poor ships and sailors
Meet their watery grave.

He shoots invincible lightning
From his fiery mouth.
He strikes more poor sailors,
The bolts zoom north, east, west and south.

When the beast slowly dies down,
The sailors dread the next few years or so.
When the mighty sea dragon rises again
And the terrifying waves will grow.

Gareth Hughes (10)
St Luke's CE Primary School, Formby

WORKING ON THE HAYSTACK

Working on the haystack, oh what a lot of fun.
Heaving up the bundles, working in the sun.
Knee-deep in this soft straw, then I hear the awesome roar.
Fred is sitting up white as chalk, Johnny's pierced him with the fork.

Jamie Teasdale (11)
St Luke's CE Primary School, Formby

POLAR BEAR

The polar bear is as soft
and white as snow.
The icicles are as sharp as
the polar bear's
claws.
It roars like the wind
blowing in the
storm.

It runs as fast
as the snow
falling.
As it sleeps on the
snow you
can't tell
which is the snow
and which is
the polar bear.

Rachael Delic (10)
St Luke's CE Primary School, Formby

THE OSTRICH

The ostrich runs like the wind,
It moves so swiftly across the land,
Hurrying rapidly over the sand,
Flattening everything in its way,
Under the hot sun throughout the day.

Emma Cookson (10)
St Luke's CE Primary School, Formby

WINTER

Winter is like
The cold North Pole.
Icicles
Are as sharp as swords.
The cold wind
Is howling like a wolf.
The snow is like
A white carpet.
Winter is as cold
As the freezing
Atlantic ocean.
The trees are as bare as
House bricks.
The world is covered
With white, white snow.

Melanie Hughes (10)
St Luke's CE Primary School, Formby

THE WIND

The wind is an owl,
The breeze is as gentle as the owl's wings,
It whistles as the bird tries to sing.
In the winter it flaps its wings,
To get off icicles and things.

Mandy Shanks (10)
St Luke's CE Primary School, Formby

THE HAYSTACK

Golden straw crunching
From somewhere, some place.
It's only the lonely farmer.
Sun glistening on children's faces.
Tasting fresh air in my nose.
The straw makes my mouth sweet.
Suddenly clouds cover the sun,
Frederick starts dancing,
No don't do it,
Mister Johnny struck Frederick with
His fork.
Frederick shouted,
His hand cut.
Later felt lonely.

Howard Hughes (10)
St Luke's CE Primary School, Formby

THE MOON

The moon is shining
Like silver,
Like a big fat ball,
Like a brilliant rock.
The moon shines very bright
In the dark,
Dark night.

Helena Seddon (8)
St Luke's CE Primary School, Formby

THE LION

The lion is like the sun,
Mighty and powerful.
Its golden mane
Is like the radiance of the sun.
The sun goes slowly round the Earth,
Like the pads of the lion's paws,
Plodding along the African plain.

Laura Telfer (10)
St Luke's CE Primary School, Formby

THE PUMA

The puma is unstoppable like the sports car.
Fast and speedy the puma goes.
The puma roars so loud.
The puma's coat is shiny like gold.
The puma is designed like the sports car.
The puma is powerful and mega-fast.
The puma is so fast you can hardly keep up with it.

Adam Churchill (9)
St Luke's CE Primary School, Formby

THE MOON

The moon is a silver round ball,
In space, far, far away,
Like the sun that shines bright,
Like the bright sunlight,
Like a round face.

Jennie Mandelkow (8)
St Luke's CE Primary School, Formby

THE MOON

The moon shines
Like a silver ball,
It glitters like the stars,
Like a stream of fresh water.
The moon is like a silver plate,
Like a land of crystals,
And diamonds.

Catherine Nixon (8)
St Luke's CE Primary School, Formby

THE SWEEPING HEDGEHOG

The hedgehog is a sweeping brush,
The slow hedgehog as brown as chocolate
sweeps up leaves on his spikes.
On a cold, dark night,
sometimes you can hear the snuffling,
sweeping noise of the hedgehog.

Jonathan Edwards (10)
St Luke's CE Primary School, Formby

THE PLANE

The plane is an eagle.
The front point of the plane is the eagle's huge beak.
The pilot's window is the eagle's eyes spying on prey.
The plane's wings are the eagle's wings keeping them in flight.
The landing wheels are the eagle's feet landing from the sky.
The end point of the plane is the eagle's tuft guarding the eagle's feet.

Rachael Karran (10)
St Luke's CE Primary School, Formby

THE MOON

The moon is
A silver circle
Made of cheese.
It is a shiny coin
Waiting to be taken to the shop.
It is a silver spoon
Flying into space.
The moon is
A silver star.
The moon is
A white bright light
Floating
In the big black
Space.

James Edwards (8)
St Luke's CE Primary School, Formby

THE SUN

The sun is a cuddly hamster,
A hamster so warm it feels,
The Earth rotates the sun,
As the hamster rotates its wheel.

The sun is as yellow as gold,
And like the hamster,
It is brave and bold.

Jack Barrett-Rosindale (10)
St Luke's CE Primary School, Formby

LOST LOVE

In the golden hay I stand,
Surrounded in this golden land.
The sun is beaming on me,
Like an eternal light.
The peace and quiet,
What could spoil this magnificent day?
A death-defying scream.
Clouds of darkness and worriedness
Descend around me.
Hearts beating like a machine.
Fred dancing around the kind
Mr Johnny, screaming, but then
It is over, I hear cries of
Sadness.

Craig Hallam (11)
St Luke's CE Primary School, Formby

THE MOON

The moon
Is a shiny silver button.
The moon
Is a torch in the dark.
The moon shines its light
On the Earth,
And lights up
The dark blue sky.

Stephanie Wrennall (8)
St Luke's CE Primary School, Formby

THE EMPTY FIELD

A hot day of harvesting
Stacking the hay,
All of us were playing
For most of the day.

Albert screamed
'Here comes the fear.'
Mister Johnny beamed
'Don't come near.'

The empty field
Such a tragic sight.
What we all feel
Is terrible fright.

Nicky Aspinwall (11)
St Luke's CE Primary School, Formby

THE MOON

The moon is
Round and shiny.
The moon is
Like a piece of cheese.
The sun shines on the moon,
The moon shines on me.
The moon is
A bright light
At night.

Lindsey Willis (8)
St Luke's CE Primary School, Formby

THE RABBIT

The rabbit is like cotton wool,
warm and fluffy.
Pads on a rabbit's feet
like the fluffiness of it stamped down.
Bouncy cotton wool as fluffy
as a rabbit's tail.
Tiny balls of cotton wool,
as small as a rabbit's gleaming eyes.
Its coat feels as if it's cotton wool
just come out of the pack.
A newborn rabbit the size of a
piece of cotton wool.

Kyndra McKinney (10)
St Luke's CE Primary School, Formby

THE STARFISH

The starfish is an icicle.
It clings to the coral like an
Icicle clinging to the window-sill.
The starfish's five pointy fingers
Are the sharp pointy icicle tips.
The cold, wet, slippery icicle,
Is a cold, wet, slippery starfish.
The starfish glides along the coral
Like the icicle slowly melting.

Roisin McIvor (9)
St Luke's CE Primary School, Formby

IN THE HAY FIELDS

It's harvest time, the sun is bright,
It's a wonderful thing to see the sight.
The golden straw lies on the floor,
Then in the distance are screaming roars
Of Frederick teasing old Johnny boy.
The anger in Mr Johnny's eyes,
Make me want to moan and cry.
Johnny scowled and picked up the fork,
Poked it at old Freddie's shorts.
Screams of death are in the air,
It's just too much for me to bear.

David Pope (11)
St Luke's CE Primary School, Formby

THE SEA HORSE

The sea is a giant white horse,
Galloping along,
His mane flying out behind him,
Splashing foam everywhere,
On stormy nights he gallops at top speed,
Making waves fly high and boats rock,
Yet, on quiet days he is sleeping
Down on his bed of seaweed,
Waiting until it is time to rise to the surface again.

Lucy Wathan (9)
St Luke's CE Primary School, Formby

SHINING SUN, YELLOW-GOLD

Shining sun, yellow-gold,
People chopping I've been told.
Hay smelling very strong,
Something goes horribly wrong.
Hitting, thumping breaks out,
Hear someone give a shout.
Dark clouds gathering in the sky,
Someone saying goodbye.
Everything starts to calm down,
There's nobody around.

Amy Begley (11)
St Luke's CE Primary School, Formby

TIGER SHARK

The tiger shark is a submarine gliding through
the murky waters.
Children are playing on a beach as bright as
the sun in summer,
Until they scream as loud as a car horn when
they spot a periscope-fin poking out of the sea.
The shark needs no torpedo.
To kill he uses his teeth as sharp as razors.
The shark growls like machinery.

Gavin Jones (10)
St Luke's CE Primary School, Formby

THE DREAM I HAD LAST NIGHT

Last night I dreamt that I had been shot up into space.
When I landed I was on Mars and I had an alien race.
Then I had a party with the aliens and we danced
                                    in the light of the moon,
Then I got back in the rocket and went back down to Earth, *zoom!*
Down on Earth I was with my mum, I had landed in Spain,
Wow! That was quick, I didn't have to go on a plane!
I dived in the pool . . . it was really cool!
As I went down, the pool seemed to grow,
So I swam up to the top and I was riding on a rainbow!
Down I went to the bottom and I found a pot of gold!
Wow! It is really true that it's not just a tale to be told?
Then I landed with a bump and I awoke
It seems as if my dreams disappeared like smoke.

Kerrie Jones (10)
St Teresa's RC Primary School, St Helens

MY LITTLE ROBOT

Oil is dripping on the floor, my little robot is no more.
I like the way he made me sing, playing games of everything.
We played at night, we played at day,
It made us both feel bright and gay.
We played games at the park,
Walking alone in the dark.
The happy times we shared together,
Now he's gone away forever.

Mark McNicholas (10)
St Teresa's RC Primary School, St Helens

ON MY WAY TO WALES

On my way to Wales in the back seat of my car,
We go along the motorway, still got to travel very far.
We go past lorries, trucks and other cars too,
And then we stop at the services because we all need the loo.
Up and down the hills we go,
Not too fast and not too slow.
Around the corners and along the straights,
Hurry up Dad we mustn't be late.
We go past lots of fields full of cows and sheep,
And on the journey home I often fall asleep.

Alison Waring (10)
St Teresa's RC Primary School, St Helens

MY BROTHER AND HIS FOOTBALL

My brother's name is Joe
and he's mad about football.
He plays it in the kitchen,
in the lounge,
and in the hall.
His favourite team's United,
and he plays like Cantona,
but whenever he gets tackled
he cries *ooah, ooah!*

Helen Alexander (10)
St Teresa's RC Primary School, St Helens

THE STARS

I look out of my window and look at the stars,
The deep black sea that leads up to Mars.
Shooting stars and alien cars,
You hear the strum of steel guitars.
The moon all shadowy, misty and grey,
It waits behind the sun till the end of the day.
All the stars glistening and the lights of the town,
All the mirrors reflecting the dew on the ground.
But then the dawn comes and into the day,
Then to Australia the stars go away.

Clare Owen (10)
St Teresa's RC Primary School, St Helens

WALKING ALONE IN THE DARK

The trees like a bird watching,
The grass like a green carpet,
The leaves like a soft feather,
The sky like a black quilt.

Mathew Taylor (10)
St Teresa's RC Primary School, St Helens

WALKING ALONE IN THE DARK

The trees are rustling in the wind,
The grass is like black spikes.
The trees are dark like a vampire's cave.
The cars sound like a wolf growling at the moon.

Liam Jones (10)
St Teresa's RC Primary School, St Helens

WALKING ALONE IN THE DARK

The trees are like a door
The trees sound like wind.
They rattle like a rattlesnake
The trees are like Blackpool tower.

Daniel Brown (10)
St Teresa's RC Primary School, St Helens

THE SLIDE

A slide is like the Winter Olympic ski run,
A slide is like a slippy snake,
When the kids go down the slide,
It takes your breath away.

John Worthington (11)
St Teresa's RC Primary School, St Helens

PETS

I have a little puppy dog,
He's always bright and gay.
I take him for a walk,
Nearly every day.

He sits down very boldly,
And watches the TV,
But when I start to eat my cake,
He turns to stare at me.

He starts to dribble,
He starts to drool,
And ends up sliding
In a pool!

Kirsty Holden (10)
St Theresa's RC Primary School, St Helens

DREAM GARDENS

Grass is like green worms
dancing in the moonlight,
A green sea of jid-didding waves.
Baby flowers walla-blubbing
about wanting to be fed.
Grass is like an enchanted mint ice-cream
running away from the spoon.

The caterpillar is like jelly
snodder-lapping across the grass.
A ladybird is like a strawberry ice-cream
covered with chocolate chips.
A spider is like a blob of hair
that has fallen out of the head.
A butterfly is like a feather gliding
through the sky with its newly opened wings.

A rose is like a red creased T-shirt
scrunched into a ball
with a long green stick up its sleeve.
The daffodil is like a long trumpet
With a green woollen thread stuck beneath it.
A tulip is like an upside-down trumpet
that calls down all the butterflies.

Natasha Roberts (11)
St Theresa's Primary School, St Helens

IT'S NOT MY FAULT

'We couldn't have done it!
We couldn't have won!'
Said the defender to the coach.
'You see, John never wore the underpants.
The lucky ones . . . you know?
It's not our fault that we lost 19-0,
You can just put the blame of Bill!
He never scored, not one goal!
He never gives his heart and soul.'
'Well then Joe, it wasn't your fault!
You only scored 13 own goals,
And broke our keeper's leg!
Oh no, Joe, it's not your fault,
You gave away 5 penalties
And got a yellow card!
It's never your fault!'
'I'm leaving and not coming back!
Find another player, Mac!'
'Ok, Joe. I'll do just that!
You horrible, spoiled little brat!'

Gary Donnelly (10)
St Theresa's RC Primary School, St Helens

SUPERSTAR

I wish I was a superstar standing on the stage,
The very next day you're on the front page.

I wish I was a superstar, how wonderful it would be,
Having my own mansion, having my own key.

I wish I was a *superstar*,
Yep, that's what I wish to be!

Dannielle Helsby (11)
St Theresa's RC Primary School, St Helens

LIVERPOOL

They're simply the best,
Way better than all the rest.
I watch 'em every time they play,
They don't just stand there
Like wet lumps of clay.

The whistle blows and off they go,
McManaman got a knock on the head,
And it got a little sore.
So off he went with a big round dent,
Whisked off into the medical tent.

So Owen came on
While McManamam had gone.
Everyone cheered
But Owen feared.

It was then 3-2 to us,
Then I went home on the bus.
I went straight to bed,
'Cos I felt dead,
And that was the end of the match.

Kerrie Johnson (11)
St Theresa's RC Primary School, St Helens

MONKEYS

If I was a monkey
Just like you
I'd jump and dance
And itch like you.

If I was a monkey
Just like you
I'd stand on my head
And stay there like glue.

If I was a monkey
Just like you
I'd swing on a tree
And hang around with you.

If I was a monkey
Just like you
I'd dance and jump
And itch like you.

Alison Hatton (11)
St Theresa's Primary School, St Helens

SPACE

Space is high, so high in the sky
It is felt-tip black
and if you run out of oxygen you won't come back
We float around in mid air
like we just don't care
We see a big meteor, it is very hot
We look at the tiny stars and there are a lot
We see the sun, it is very bright
We go a little closer and I say
'I think it is a bit too light!'
We see the Earth so wonderful and round
And then some aliens that have never been found
We see a Milky Way, it looks delicious
But oh no! There is an asteroid and
it looks vicious.

Andrew Seagraves (10)
St Winefride's Juniors, Bootle

WAR POEM

On goes the siren
We go to the bomb shelter
The German bombs come through the sky
Then we see people lie
Either injured or even dead
Through the streets we are led
Some people doubting
Others shouting
Running for our lives
Like a goalkeeper dives
When will the war be over?
Then we can go to Dover
Go see Aunty Lou and Uncle Dave
Then to Wookey Hole Cave
Off goes the siren and we are safe, or are we?

Stephen Ford (9)
St Winefride's Juniors, Bootle

PASSOVER POEM

Moses, the man who led the way,
Over a night and endless day.
Innocents saved at the time
of the great,
Escape from Egyptian land,
Soon they will be free.

Frankie McKeon (10)
St Winefride's Juniors, Bootle

THE ROLLER-COASTER

R oller-coasters are fun
O ther people riding up and down with you
L ouder and louder people scream
L ower and higher you go
E very roller-coaster has bumps
R olling up and down hills like jumping up and down
C old, wet, sunny or dry they still go faster
O ut comes screaming
A nd shouting
S hould you go alone?
T hey all go very fast
E ven though you don't like them
R oller-coasters are great.

Stephanie Evans (10)
St Winefride's Juniors, Bootle

ASTRONAUT

I want to be an astronaut
Float around all day
Go to Mars, play on stars
And come back home in May.

I want to be an astronaut
Flying in the sky
Play guitar and sing 'Ha ha.'
Music from on high.

Daniel Sullivan (10)
St Winefride's Juniors, Bootle

CHRISTMAS EVENING

Snow is falling on the ground,
Can you hear the cheerful sound?
People sing a happy song,
Knowing nothing can go wrong.

Presents under the Christmas tree,
I hope one of them is for me.
Parties and dances here and there,
Everyone has that Christmas care.

Christmas cards are all sent,
But when they get there they are all bent.
All the Christmas lights are on,
When we wake up Santa is gone.

Jayne Tomley (10)
St Winefride's Juniors, Bootle

SOUTHPORT

S outhport was very exciting when we got there.
O n the way to the Fun House everybody was talking about the rides.
U nusual how the Black Hole works.
T he Black Hole was our first fright.
H urrying to the next amazing ride.
P eople were scared of the huge Pirate Ship.
O ur second to last fright was the Ghost Train.
R ushing to get off it for the next shock.
T he last ride was the Cyclone, the scariest for me.

Craig Graham (10)
St Winefride's Juniors, Bootle

THE DELICATE FLOWER

The soft gentle flower like a
warm summer's breeze,
hungry butterflies coming,
satisfied butterflies going. But
if you look closely, very closely
indeed, you will see all the
colours merging together like
a wonderful magic spell, it
really is like going into
another world of peace,
happiness, love of one
another and no suffering.

Sarah Groom (11)
St Winefride's Juniors, Bootle

SOUTHPORT

S outport fair was amazing!
O h, look at the great rides.
U p and down, round and round
T ill they stop
H igh in the grey sky.
P irate ship was great
O n the crazy Cyclone
R oller-coaster big and fast
T ill the amazing ride is over.

Kerry Jones (10)
St Winefride's Juniors, Bootle

SOUTHPORT FAIR

S low rides, fast rides
O h no! What am I going to do?
U p and down they all go to
T he Pirate Ship went higher than a house
H ere and there I hear the quiet mouse
P eople screaming louder and louder
O h, I really think I am getting an earache!
R eally think the Cyclone is crazy and as fast as could be
T he Cyclone goes higher and higher, when you
    go up in the sky you can see the sea.

Chelsee Cousins (10)
St Winefride's Juniors, Bootle

IF

If, there was no pollution
the Earth would be a better place.

If, the rainforest trees were not cut down
the Earth would be a better place.

If, new species could be found
the Earth would be a better place.

If, people didn't have to be in poverty
the Earth would be a better place.

If, peace could be between countries
the Earth would be a better place.

If, there was no anger and hate
the Earth would be a better place.

Philip Lennon (10)
Shoreside Primary School

NO ONE AGREES

Everyone sees things differently
No one agrees anymore
The whole world has become a big debate
Has power ruined it all?

The affluent sleep on beds of money
While others sleep on stone
The world relies on the one at the top
No feelings the rich man shows

While the world is falling on its knees
The leaders just start a war
Does no one know what's happening here?
Has agreement hit the floor?

'When will it end?' cry the sufferers
'Why does it happen to me?'
'When will what end?' cry the wealthy
'I'm counting my money can't you see?'

Time flies by and people shout
'Does no one know what it's all about?
People can fly to Mars,
We can reach the stars!'

'Why would you want to do that?' the lonely say
'I just want a home,
If science and statistics rule the world
then work out how many people are all alone.'

People try and find the meaning of life
Shouldn't we sort life out first?
People sit there swimming in wealth
While others are dying of thirst.

Steven Forshaw (10)
Shoreside Primary School

THE BUSHY RED TAIL

The vixen wakes and sniffs the air
She comes out of her home taking care
That her steps are light as they pad on the ground
But in the distance she hears a deadly sound,
The sound of fox-hunters is quite near
She realizes she must lead them away from here,
Away from her cubs that lay snuggled in bed
If she waits a moment later they'll soon be dead
So with a flick of her tail and a wave of farewell
She dashes away faster than hell.
With a face full of worry, a face full of fright
She comes darting out into the light
As the dogs see her they start on the trail
And never lose sight of the bushy red tail.
The mother fox is sly and quick
But the hunting dogs know her trick,
To run over the fields and into the lane
To get lost in the bushes, she won't be seen again.
The mother fox begins to lag
And the dogs gain power in their game of tag.
A pain shoots through the vixen's heart
As her whole body is torn apart.
She lets out her last sad groan,
To the five fox cubs left home alone . . .

Emma Chandley (10)
Shoreside Primary School

THE LAND

I see the leaves fluttering by.
I swim the ocean as the birds fly.
I sit on the rocks as the sky drops with darkness.
The sand between my toes; the trees sway their
branches.

Dawn comes to the morning blaze.
I look at the pale blue skies. I gaze.
It's just so beautiful, I don't want to leave.
The sea tide comes in the dream I weave.

Harriet Aitken (10)
Shoreside Primary School

THE SEASONS

Summer's gone,
The Earth's covered in leaves,
Here comes autumn,
With a chilly cold breeze,
With Hallowe'en and a fireworks show,
Eating toffee all wrapped in a bow,
But as soon as it's over,
Along comes winter,
At the beginning it's warm,
But then it gets colder,
Jack Frost is around waiting till nightfall,
All the houses are covered in a white ice wall,
The birds return with their song so gay,
Winter has gone,
Spring's here.
Hooray!
The bulbs go in,
Mothered by the sun,
They grow into flowers,
The Earth has won,
Summer has come with more happiness to share,
Play all day with laughter and cheer,
But as soon as it's come,
It's gone and winter is here!

Jenny Hearnshaw (11)
Shoreside Primary School

WHAT IS AN ALIEN?

What does an alien look like?
Has it got guns?
Is it green and slimy?
Has it got loads of eyes?
Does it have a mouth?
Can it talk?
Is it anything like a humanoid?
Who knows.

What does an alien do in its life?
Does it work in a restaurant?
Has it got loads of money?
Do aliens have money?
Does it do business?
Are they friends with each other?
Who knows.

Where does an alien live?
Does it live in a house on planet Mars?
Does it live on a planet or an asteroid or a comet?
Who knows, maybe we'll find out?
Who knows.

Hannah McBride (11)
Shoreside Primary School

POMPEII

Blood, gas, rocks and madness in Pompeii,
Vesuvius banging and roaring,
People are dying in pain and suffering,
Homes covered with mud and lava,
Everyone dies.

Gary Menzies (8)
Shoreside Primary School

THE RABBITS ON WATERSHIP DOWN

Over hedges, through a bush,
Rabbits feeding, quite a hush.
Noses twitching in the dew,
Rabbits resting beneath the yew,
Listening to the blackbird's trill.
Winter is coming, the air is chill.
Down a burrow, sandy floor,
Rabbits lend a helping paw.
It is dark but the rabbits don't mind,
All they think of is being kind.
Down to a nest of grass and hay,
'May we peek?'
'Yes you may.'
Baby bunnies have been born,
A nest of fur, it keeps them warm.
The circle of life, it starts again,
But Zorn means destruction, Zorn means rain.
They'll grow up to be quite strong,
Let's hope their life is extra long.

Martha Sprackland (9)
Shoreside Primary School

WHAT IF?

What if the sun was really small?
What if the moon was very tall?
What if all the planets were square?
What if the Earth wasn't there?
What if all these things were true?
What if it was?
Would it harm me and you?

Jenna McKenna (11)
Shoreside Primary School

THE SUN

The sun is a red fireball up in the sky,
A great big eye watching me,
A pancake tossed and stuck in space,
A beaming, smiley face looking at me,
It is a great big hot wheel floating in the air,
An enormous torch lighting up the sky,
The sun is a great big bee buzzing up high,
A golden egg laid by a golden goose,
The sun is a big red football,
Kicked round the world,
Someone is looking for it,
I don't know who,
A burning balloon floating in the air,
But at night it has gone,
Hello moon, goodnight sun,
Then twelve hours pass,
Hello sun, goodbye moon!

Jenny Owen (9)
Shoreside Primary School

POMPEII

B-bbb bang!
Skies go black,
A giant flame on the hill.
What shall I do? Go this way or that?
Mum, Mum, where are you?
What a horror, I can't breathe.
I feel unsteady
And I'm about to collapse and die.

Daniel Trickett (9)
Shoreside Primary School

MY RABBIT, MR NIBBLES

Hear the rabbit munching away
Looking around for his best food
Tomatoes, carrots, cucumber too
And that's how he likes it.
When I come up to him
He sniffs me and then licks me
He says to himself 'Take me out, take me out'
But he does not speak, only a clicking noise
To show his happiness
And that's how he likes it.
Separating his mat on my lap
Gets comfy and takes a nap.
In his run he runs around exercising his legs
Bites the lino, moves his toys, and arranges his materials
So that's how he likes it.

Bryony Beale (8)
Shoreside Primary School

HAUNTED HOUSE

As I went into the haunted house,
The floor began to creak,
The witches did their magic spells,
And the ghosts began to speak,
With goblins' tongues and wizards' hats,
I couldn't take much more of that.
I ran outside,
The floor fell in,
I jumped in the car and went for a spin.

Jenna Davidson (10)
Shoreside Primary School

ALIENS ON THE MOON

As I walked on the moon,
I saw
Lifeless rocks
Lifeless craters
Dead dust
Bright stars zooming by.
Other planets looked like stars
In the vast open space
All was quiet, all was black.
I also saw,
Two bright green aliens with scales
As skin and no arms or legs,
And some water.
Hang on, did I say
       Aliens?

Adam Cadwell (10)
Shoreside Primary School

WEATHER IS ESSENTIAL

The Earth spins in outer space.
The clouds gather water to rain all over the place.
Let the water splash on your face.
Be thankful for the weather,
For without it life on Earth would cease.
Plants and people too would die,
Without water or warmth.
Even the wind helps us too.
Please help us sustain our planet
Please do.

Anne Marie Watson (11)
Shoreside Primary School

FIREWORKS

10, 9, 8, 7, 6, 5, 4, 3, 2, 1, 0,
Bangers, rockets blast off into the dark, bright
colours light the sky
sparklers sparkling in the dark. Bangers banging
like a shotgun.
Rockets whistling and then a big bang!

Bangs and screeches you hear at night
the twirling and whizzing of the Catherine wheel
keeps you awake.
The screams of screamers fill the night.
Fireworks, fireworks at night.
Wiggly worms zigzagging like mouse tails
Chinese crackers are like jumping grasshoppers.
Fireworks, fireworks in the middle of the night.

Daniel Green (9)
Shoreside Primary School

HAMSTERS

It's seven o'clock and they've just uncurled,
They yawn, their mouths looking as if they've swallowed the world.
They run around meeting each other and having a chat,
They sit side by side. They really look fat.
They hide in the corner and jog in the wheel,
Then run away for a bit of a meal.
They all look like friends,
With a tiny tail at rear ends.
I do love my hamsters, they are very sweet,
When I'm up every morning they're here for me to greet.

Philip Ratcliffe (10)
Shoreside Primary School

WHERE DOES YOUR MONEY GO?

Where does your money go
When you spend £8000 on a car?
To a fat, wealthy shop owner
Or the malnourished poor?

Where does your money go
When you buy a new dress?
To the malevolent manager
Or the half-naked homeless?

Where does your money go
When you go on a vacation?
To the ecstatic travel agent
Or people trapped in darkness?

Where does your money go?

Rhona Morris (11)
Shoreside Primary School

DROWNED BY FRIDGES

Things like refrigerators,
Cars and radiators,
Are making holes in the ozone,
Everyone must hear, it shall be known.
The icecap is melting, far to the north,
And all the seas shall come gushing forth,
So a lot of people at a seaside town,
Will all be washed away, we'll drown,
So shut off your fridge and buy a new one,
Or everyone will die, we'll all be gone.

Michael Hall (11)
Shoreside Primary School

ALONE

I sat alone on the bench,
Staring at me were their frightening eyes,
I wondered why I was alone that day,
Then it all came back,
We had a row that turned into a fight,
I came off worst,
The words they said,
Hurt me deep inside,
They were worse than punching or kicking,
They hurt me more as they took my friends away,
Then a girl came up to me,
And picked up my spirits,
Now I don't need my old friends,
I've got a new one who likes me.

Jenna Gavin (11)
Shoreside Primary School

THE TREE-FROG

There's a glow of green at the top of the trees,
What could it be that everyone sees?
It has bright yellow eyes and a long pink tongue,
From a large green leaf it is hung.
It is the tree-frog that everyone spies,
He is munching away at all the flies.
But people are cutting down his home
And home is the only place to roam.
Not much longer and the tree-frog will be gone,
Now there's a few left, soon there'll be none.

Stephanie Jayson (10)
Shoreside Primary School

ANNOYED!

'Who do you think you are?
Flying to *our* moon!
You've been around *our* galaxy!
We know you'll be back soon!
Yes! Just in 30 years from now you'll be
living on *our* moon!
You selfish things!
You don't think about us!
We don't have *our* own bedroom!
So it's just a little warning that you're *not*
welcome here to stay.
So maybe . . . in a year or so . . .
We'll be visiting Earth!
. . . What do *you* say? . . . '

Alexandra March (10)
Shoreside Primary School

WHAT I BELIEVE

I don't know what to believe
My mind is in a twist.

                     Does Father Christmas
                     Eat our pies, or is he a fat old phoney?

Do we come back
As something else
Or lie in our graves forever?

                     Are there fairies or angels
                     That look down on us?

Will I ever find out?

                     I'll have to wait and see.

Matthew Dent (11)
Shoreside Primary School

RABBITS

It's early morning. I get out of bed,
I rub my eyes and scratch my head.
I open the window, take a breath of fresh air,
I put on my specs and I see out there,
a boring old field and some birds in the sky,
and suddenly a creature, incredibly shy.
First the head, then the feet and a sweet fluffy tail,
it ran like the wind down its own little trail.
One minute later there was 1000 or more,
all darting round on the cold winter's floor.
I ran downstairs and put on my coat,
they were jumping so high, I thought they could float.
I ran to the fence, took a huge leap,
but all I could see were a few old sheep.

Edward Greenwood (11)
Shoreside Primary School

THE SPACE AROUND US

We live in a space,
A space of stars, planets and moons,
A space of life and a space of death.
We live on a planet,
A planet called Earth,
But if we don't let it live,
Where shall we go?
We might go to Mars,
We might go to the Moon.
But wherever we go
It's not like the Earth we once knew.

Michael Scholfield (10)
Shoreside Primary School

TWILIGHT OF NATURE

Mother Nature looks over us
And watches helplessly while man destroys her.
The air is no longer crisp and fresh
It is scented with greed and hate.
Men are too comfortable and ignorant to notice
That they are destroying their home.
Factories keep on polluting,
The Earth becomes more frail.
Every day the ozone layer is deteriorating,
But men's hunger for comfort and enjoyment
Has possessed their minds.
Our extinction is inevitable,
Unless man repairs the damage he has done.

Andrew Rea (10)
Shoreside Primary School

ABOVE THE CLOUDS

Beyond the clouds, above the trees
Way past the stars and galaxies
A little spaceship boldly flew
Far away from me and you.
A tiny speck all on its own
Amongst the stars its engines drone
On its path the craft continues
Its occupants look out the windows.
All of this is going on
Beyond the clouds, above the trees
Way past the stars and galaxies.

James Fitzgerald (11)
Shoreside Primary School

IF I COULD CHANGE

If I could change the Earth,
I'd make it special,
I'd make it clean,
I'd make it free,
I'd give it all the love from me.
It's our world,
It's our life,
We live on the Earth
So let it be.
If you could change the Earth right now,
It would be true
Because the Earth is me and the
Earth is you.

Hannah Brownlow (9)
Shoreside Primary School

THE EARTH

Volcanoes smashing and crashing
Dinosaurs roaring and snoring.
That was before.
This is now.
Time passes by as the Earth goes round.
No smashing and crashing
And definitely no roaring.
But if we don't help the Earth
It will go boring.
Save the Earth from dying,
Because if we don't the human race will go flying.

Andrew Dodson (10)
Shoreside Primary School

WONDERING

For thousands of years people have wondered,
'What's out there, what's out there in the blackness?
Is it a giant beetle rolling some silver dung?
Or is it a man being eaten by monsters?'
For thousands of years people have wondered,
'What is that silver ball?'
For thousands of years people have wondered,
'What are those silvery specks?
Are they ancient heroes full of glory?
Or are they ancient demons hung for eternity?'
For thousands of years people have wondered,
but now we know.
       Or do we?

Maximilian Bienkowski (11)
Shoreside Primary School

THE EARTH

The Earth is our friend,
The Earth is our barrier.
The Earth means life,
The Earth means love.
The Earth carries health,
The Earth carries sickness.
The Earth deserves better,
The Earth deserves help.
The Earth has a right,
The Earth lives.
The Earth is round,
The Earth should be around forever.

Jennifer Gorrell (9)
Shoreside Primary School

THE EMPTY HOUSE

In a dark corner of an old empty house
There lived a spider and a mouse
They had lived in the house for fifteen long years
And in that time they had both shed some tears

The house was so quiet, lonely and cold
They huddled together until they grew old
Then came the day when the spider said 'Mouse
I can't live much longer in this cold empty house'

The very next day when they awoke from their sleep
The mouse looked at the spider and thought he looked weak
The mouse took hold of the spider and put him on his back
He started to walk down an old pony track

The mouse had been walking for hours and hours
He came to a house with a garden full of flowers
The spider looked up and said 'This is the one
We will spend the rest of our days here and have a bit of fun.'

Scott Jewkes Keating (10)
Stanney Grange CP School

WEATHER

Most of the time it's raining,
We spend most of our time moaning,
It rains most of the time in winter,
The sun shines most of the time in summer,
In autumn all of the leaves fall off the trees,
Sometimes the wind knocks us on our knees.

Karen Duffin (10)
Stanney Grange CP School

THE KNIGHT AND THE DRAGON

People surrounding stick fires at night,
Tucking into their barbecued feasts.
Telling of magical stories of old about heroes
                        and mythical beasts.

This scene that is set,
In this fable they tell, is a town under siege,
Its folk suffering terror and fright,
From a gigantic beast with fire for breath,
And glowing eyes that pierce the night.

The horrible monster,
The villain of peace,
Is a dragon,
The biggest you could meet.
He burns all the houses,
And eats all the folk,
To him they are titbits, just treats.

The days are filled with horror,
The nights are filled with pain.
Not sleeping in your bed at night in fear the
                        monster may come again.

But out of the mist and the rain,
And into the horror and pain,
Comes a knight in shining armour,
Is this man a fool?
On his trusty steed,
With his sword at his side,
Through the wake of destruction he rides.

He engages the monster in a titanic battle,
With a slash of his shining sword,
The monster has a taste of his metal.

The beast falls to the ground,
People crowd all around,
But with a roar the dragon gets up from the floor,
People scatter.

With a huff and a puff
The fearless knight is covered in flames,
His shining armour in tatters.

With another huff and a flash
And an almighty clash
The brave knight no longer matters.

Sam Fry (11)
Stanney Grange CP School

WE ARE ALL DIFFERENT

Long pointy fingers.
Little button nose.
Big pouty lips.
Long stubby toes.
Some people tall.
And some people small.
Some men have beards.
Women not at all.
Some people fat
And some people thin.
Some hair long and some hair trim.
Everyone is different,
Every step they take each day.
Everyone is different
In their own special way!

Claire Hall (11)
Stanney Grange CP School

WINTER

Winter is a cold time of year,
Sometimes it snows,
It is cold in the winter everyone knows,
Animals are hibernating, waiting for summer to come,
Humans are inside getting warm by the fire,
The sun has faded away,
The darkness has come,
Rainy dull weather,
It's no fun!

Abigail Jones (10)
Stanney Grange CP School

BIG AND BLUE

I'm a whale I'm big and blue,
I live in the ocean unlike you.
Trawlers fish by day and night,
Draining the food, that can't be right.
So cast your nets but let some through,
For future generations it's up to you.
But after all I'm just a whale,
With no fish, life will fail.

Nikki Mather (10)
Stanney Grange CP School

THE GREEN CROSS CODE

If you think about crossing the road
You should always use the Green Cross Code.
Look left
Look right
Then if there's nothing in sight
Cross with care.
Be careful, beware
Do not stare, there could be a car
Just there.

Kelly Dunkerley (11)
Stanney Grange CP School

THE LIZARD

I am the mean green mowing machine.
People say that I am green.
I like to eat things that are green.
I don't believe that I am green.
I looked in the mirror and found out
That I was green. I am green.
I said to myself 'I've got a big long tail
And some spikes on my back.'
I am a lizard.

Jodie Seymour (10)
Stanney Grange CP School

HENRY VIII

Henry VIII was very very fine
He liked to eat and drink lots of wine
He had six wives
Wife number one
Was Catherine of Aragon

Anne Boleyn was number two
She lost her head when her days were through
She had her baby Good Queen Beth
But even that didn't save her from death

Jane Seymour was wife number three
She was as happy as could be
When she had a new baby boy
But soon she was to have no joy

Anne of Cleeves was number four
It wasn't long before she was shown the door
Like number one she kept her head
She too was divorced

Catherine Howard was number five
She didn't have long to be alive
They soon turned the key in the lock
And placed her head upon the block

Wife number six was Catherine Parr
She didn't have to travel very far
She outlived the King
And was free to do anything.

Nicholas Wood (9)
Thornton Hough Primary School

SPACE

Here came the day for us to go
And reach the shining stars,
To travel to Saturn or Jupiter
Or even go to Mars!

When we left the Earth's atmosphere
I go a funny sensation,
Of suddenly being weightless and having
To fly around the station!

We finally landed on Jupiter
We'd reached our destination,
We got on our hefty spacesuits
And started our exploration!

I felt really lonely that day
Nothing made a sound,
Radio communication was our only link
As we bounced our way around.

As we came back to Earth that week
I thought about what I'd done,
I put the first foot on Jupiter
And a different perspective of the Sun.

Gordon Farquhar (10)
Thornton Hough Primary School

OUTER SPACE

Packing my bags on my way into space
flying to the moon in perfect grace.
Into my rocket I strap myself
lift-off soon after countdown, *whoosh!*

The moon is coming into sight
when I'm on the moon I become very light.
I can see the Earth from the moon
I am going back there very soon.

I have flown back to the main rocket
we are coming back to Earth
at the speed of electricity
through a socket.

Splash! We have hit the water.
The recovery team are here
I have enjoyed my journey into space
but I much prefer my own place
                Earth!

William Parry-Jones (10)
Thornton Hough Primary School

SPACE POEM

S is for stars that shine so bright.
P is for planets you see in the night.
A is for astronaut on his space flight.
C is for comets with their tails alight.
E is for Earth, what a wonderful sight.

Christopher Hulley (10)
Thornton Hough Primary School

SPACE, THE FINAL FRONTIER

Mercury, Venus, Earth and Mars,
All in space just like the stars.
Jupiter, Saturn, Uranus and Neptune
And Pluto soon.

Red planets, yellow planets, green and blue
Neptune has an ice-cold crust
Uranus does too
Black holes, white holes, green and red
Don't! enter any of these you will end up dead.

Planets, moons, suns and stars
All much bigger than motor cars.
Stars with white dwarfs and red and yellow
Just like the one next to Mars.

Space walks and landings
So quickly it's hard to believe.
Space dinners and take-offs
10, 9, 8, 7, 6, 5, 4, 3, 2, 1.

Christopher Wood (10)
Thornton Hough Primary School

SPACE NECKLACE

Space is as black as coal.
The moons are like pearls.
The sun sparkles like a ruby.
Stars twinkle like polished diamonds.
The Earth is like a marbled gemstone
On a necklace through the sky.

Stuart Webb (9)
Thornton Hough Primary School

THE CIRCUS

I'm going to a circus on Sunday.
Just down the road from my house.
We walked down to the circus to pay.
They have elephants and camels but do they have a mouse?

Part of me says I can't wait to go,
The other part has lots of doubt.
It says on the leaflet 'Come to the show'
But I don't know if I really want to go.

It's been on my mind a lot
About the animals and the life they have got.
Are they happy or are they sad?
Is their life really that bad?

But the music that I can hear
Makes me think, don't judge until you can see.
Maybe on Sunday when I have seen the show,
I'll let you know, if you ought to go.

Sarah Taperell (11)
Thornton Hough Primary School

SPACE

As I fly through the air, towards the moon,
Higher and higher, until we touch space,
I see stars, Venus, Jupiter and Mars,
Now we're there on the Moon,
The first men to walk the white Moon,
It's quiet, dark and lonely up there.

Michael Hopkinson (10)
Thornton Hough Primary School

SNAKES

Slippery slimy snake
Slow sly snake
Creepy long snake
Slithery shaky snake
Small thin snake
Big fat snake
Slippy slimy snake

Grass snakes
Cobra snakes
Water snakes
Bush snakes
Python snakes
Rattlesnakes
Snakes!

Thomas Richardson (9)
Thornton Hough Primary School

TIGER

Tiger tiger, creeping down,
low, waiting for a zebra passing by,
the zebra passes by,
the tiger watches with its sharp yellow eye,
ready to pounce on the zebra,
with its sharp claws.

Sam Pringle (9)
Thornton Hough Primary School

SPACE

Space space
 What a wonderful place
  I would like to be.
   In a rocket you will fly
    Higher and higher in the sky.

     Yesterday, I thought, what it
      Would be like to be an astronaut
       In and out of my suit
        Oh no! I've lost a boot!

         The sun, the stars and the moon
          I will see you very soon.
           Do you know the language of Latin?
            Jupiter, Mars, Venus and Saturn.

David Griffiths (10)
Thornton Hough Primary School

TIGER

Tiger tiger, why are you so mean?
Tiger tiger, why are you so lively?
Tiger tiger, why are you so hungry?
Tiger tiger, why are you so fast?
Tiger tiger, why are you so strong?
Tiger tiger, why are you so heavy?

Matthew Davies (8)
Thornton Hough Primary School

SPACE

Space is all around us
filled with air and stars.
The planets have different names
such as Jupiter, Venus and Mars.

Neil Armstrong, Buzz Aldrin and Michael Collins
were the first men on the Moon,
They took a step and then came back,
and other ones tried again soon.

Nine planets revolve around the Sun,
and give us night and day,
We look at stars and wonder how
they all can be there and stay.

Sarah Warburton (10)
Thornton Hough Primary School

THE CATERPILLAR

Caterpillar, caterpillar, why are you so small?
Caterpillar, caterpillar, why do you crawl?
Caterpillar, caterpillar, why are you that colour?
Caterpillar, caterpillar, why do you get bigger?
Caterpillar, caterpillar, why do you eat so much?
Caterpillar, caterpillar, where have you gone?
Caterpillar, caterpillar, are you my friend?
Caterpillar, caterpillar,
                              Butterfly!

Hayley Dineley (9)
Thornton Hough Primary School

SPACE

Countdown has started
I'm in the capsule waiting to go
It's Apollo 11
That's taking me to space
Blast-off has begun
The boosters are roaring

I'm in space I can see
Stars all around me for miles
I can see the Moon not far away
And the Earth is behind me
It's amazing blue, white and green
It's great!

Michael Kenworthy (10)
Thornton Hough Primary School

UP, UP, UP AND AWAY

Higher and higher and higher I go,
Who knows what I am going to see,
I may never see Earth again,
That's what is troubling me.

I land on Jupiter
I don't see much
Except gas, and feel so hot,
I see through the gas, a tiny coloured dot,
Hang on, that's Earth, it's thousands of light years away.

Christopher Williams (9)
Thornton Hough Primary School

SPACE SHUTTLE

S is for space, that's where we are
P is for power, I can feel a lot of that
A is for astronaut, that's what I am!
C is for capsule, that's where I am
E is for exciting, that's what I feel

S is for space, we've got a lot of that
H is for how, how do I survive?
U is for Uranus, light years away
T is for tremendous, that's everything
T is for tempted, tempted to survive
L is for light, we don't see much of that
E is for extreme, this mission is extreme.

Richard Guile (10)
Thornton Hough Primary School

SPACE POEM

A is for astronaut boarding the
S huttle. And we have
T ake-off.
R ockets are exploding underneath us
O n board a spaceship in Mission Control
N ASA. The spaceship
A pollo 13. We are aiming to land on
U ranus. We are passing Saturn's largest moon
T riton. We are amazed by the size of
S tars.

Charlotte Wright (10)
Thornton Hough Primary School

SPACE POEM

5, 4, 3, 2, 1, blast-off.
I'm in my rocket going to space.
It's a very big place
I can't wait to get to space.
I'm warming up ready for space
Getting our experiment ready.
We have landed in space
We are on our space buggies.
We have got the experiment
It worked!
We had left our space buggies behind in space.
We left our English flag there.

Tom Henaghan (9)
Thornton Hough Primary School

THE TUDOR KING

H   enry was a Tudor king
E   ngland was his country
N   ot at all silly or stupid
R   eally he was quite kind
Y   uk, he ate wild boar

T   he king was quite wise and quite strong
H   onest because he wanted a son
E   normous he was but not so small

8th I think was the date of his birthday.

Alicia Khoshdel (9)
Thornton Hough Primary School

BELFAST

At the football ground
The army found
The Soviets had invaded
The army ran
To scan the Soviets.

In London near the Tower Bridge
The Belfast ran into a ridge
The Soviets had taken over London
The Belfast fired and blew Big Ben
Big Ben fell and the bell rang
The Soviets went back to Russia.

Stuart Beattie (8)
Thornton Hough Primary School

WICKED WITCHES

All witches have a dark hat,
and usually carry with them a black cat.

Most witches have a book of spells,
within the secrets they never tell.

Crooked hats, witches' cats,
all these things the witches have.
I'd love to be a witch myself
because some witches have wealth.
One of the witches was Anne Boleyn,
she was so wealthy, she married a king.

Kathryn Ashcroft (9)
Thornton Hough Primary School